Disorganized Attachment Workbook

Healing Past Wounds, Building Stability, and Cultivating Healthy Attachments for Lasting Connections

Free Bonus from Andy Gardner

Hi!

My name is Andy Gardner, and first off, I want to THANK YOU for reading my book.

Now you have a chance to join my exclusive email list related to human psychology and self-development so you can get the ebook below for free as well as the potential to get more ebooks for free! Simply click the link below to join.

P.S. Remember that it's 100% free to join the list.

Access your free bonuses here: https://livetolearn.lpages.co/andy-gardner-disorganized-attachment-workbook-paperback/

Or, Scan the QR code!

Table of Contents

Introduction

Most people you meet are wounded. They carry baggage from their past that no one else can see. However, many choose to heal and not to allow their past trauma to impact their present and future.

You are probably reading this book because you have been through a traumatic experience in your childhood, or perhaps your parents didn't know how to love you. Whatever you experienced, understand that none of it was your fault.

You are only responsible for your choices; you are here because you chose to heal.

The book begins by introducing the concept of disorganized attachment, its origin, and how it affects your adult life and relationships. You will then discover the relationship between your childhood experiences and disorganized attachment. You will understand the different attachment styles that children usually form.

You are ready to start your healing journey after understanding the concept and its impact on your life. You'll learn how to overcome your trauma and rebuild yourself. You'll also discover the power of embracing your wounds in your recovery.

People who experience disorganized attachment as children may struggle with trusting others or forming healthy bonds. You'll learn that trust is the foundation of any healthy relationship. You'll also discover its role in creating connections with people who make you feel safe and loved.

You'll then learn about the significance of communication in connecting and developing a deeper understanding of others. You will discover the significance of self-compassion and its role in your healing.

You'll understand the purpose of healthy relationships and how you can attract positive people into your life. You will learn about empathy and the ability to put yourself in other people's shoes to better relate to their struggles and pain.

You'll then learn about resilience and how to become the strongest version of yourself to handle whatever life throws your way.

The last part of the book explores the concept of a "Supportive community" and how having healthy people in your life helps you grow into the amazing person you are meant to be.

This book has all the information you need to start your recovery. All concepts are explained using simple words and examples. Each chapter has exercises and strategies with step-by-step instructions.

The road to recovery begins with a choice, and now that you have made yours, you are ready to heal and grow.

Section 1: Understanding Disorganized Attachment

Children come into this life like a blank page. They have no experience or understanding of the world. The adults in their lives shape them and are responsible for the first things they see, hear, and feel.

Some parents nourish their children and shower them with love and affection. They create a positive and safe environment for their little ones to learn and grow based on trust and respect.

Other children aren't so lucky. They grew up with parents who never knew how to love and only taught them anger, rejection, and pain. The child never learned what it meant to be cared for and accepted.

They never felt safe or comfortable in their home. All their experiences are associated with abandonment, hatred, and anxiety. The child who was never taught how to love or trust becomes an adult unable to relate to others or build healthy relationships.

Many children who grew up in dysfunctional homes carry childhood trauma into adulthood.

Your past doesn't have to define or control the person you will become. You can begin your healing journey and release the shackles weighing you down.

This section explains the concept of disorganized attachment and its origin. You'll discover real-life stories of people who had similar experiences. You will also find strategies and exercises to foster self-awareness.

What Is Disorganized Attachment?

Disorganized or fearful-avoidant attachment is characterized by inner conflict, unpredictable and inconsistent behavior, fear, and mistrust. A person with a disorganized attachment style often pursues intimacy and desires to create strong relationships and close bonds with the people in their lives.

However, when someone tries to come close and fulfill their emotional needs, they quickly detach and push this person away. They build walls around themselves to prevent anyone from seeing their vulnerability. Their fear of abandonment prevents them from connecting with others because they believe that everyone will eventually leave.

Disorganized attachment is one of the most complex and rarest types of insecure attachment. It is usually the result of an extremely traumatic childhood where a child grows up in an unstable home with emotionally abusive and unreliable caregivers. This experience can have a huge impact on how they approach relationships in their adulthood.

Origin of Disorganized Attachment

Attachment is the emotional connection and bond a person forms in early childhood with their parents or caregivers. Your relationship with your parents during your formative years determines how you will connect and relate to others throughout your life.

When an infant cries, a parent should make them feel safe and fulfill their emotional or physical needs. However, some parents are unable to provide support and comfort. If they are toxic or abusive, they can betray the child's sense of safety.

They don't just neglect their child's emotional needs but can become a threat and a source of terror. The child realizes that their attachment figure and the person they thought would protect them from the world is someone to be feared and avoided. This can be extremely confusing and traumatic.

Children seek protection from the source of their fears to alleviate another fear. For instance, you may ask your parents, who you are afraid of, to protect you from a terrifying rabid dog. This situation is called "Fright without a solution." You constantly fear your caretakers but must rely on them to survive.

When the person you trust fails you, you grow up expecting the same from everyone else. These feelings of disappointment and distrust don't go away by themselves. They stay with you, influencing your attachment style and relationships.

Other causes of disorganized attachment include sexual, verbal, emotional, or physical abuse from parents, witnessing parents abusing or harming each other or an older sibling, or emotionally unavailable parents.

Unpredictable behavior can also cause disorganized attachment. Healthy parents are usually predictable in their reactions and responses to their child's needs. Children usually thrive in a stable and consistent environment. However, when a child doesn't know how their parents will react, they will constantly feel confused as they don't know what to expect.

Interestingly, some people with disorganized attachment were never abused as children. If one or both parents suffered from unresolved trauma, they might involuntarily project their pain onto their child. For instance, if your mother lost a child, she might be too traumatized to care for you. Parents who suffer from depression or substance abuse may also showcase unpredictable behavior that leads to disorganized attachment in their child.

Signs of Disorganized Attachment

- Expecting betrayal or rejection in all of your relationships.
- Lack of trust, especially during moments when your partner is loving and supportive.
- Feeling uncomfortable when someone tries to connect with you.
- Inability to believe your partner when they say that they will always be there for you.
- Struggling to be vulnerable and opening up to others.
- Feeling unworthy of love.
- A constant desire to be close and connect to others.
- Experiencing anxiety or depression.
- Feeling deep-rooted shame.
- Low self-esteem.
- Negative thoughts.
- Fear of caregivers.
- Aggressive behavior toward the abusive parent.
- Lashing out at your partner.
- Patterns of chaotic and unpredictable behavior and relationships.
- Avoiding others.
- Fear of abandonment.
- Poor emotional regulation.
- Difficulty with opening up to others.

- Distant or clingy behavior.
- Inconsistent behavior in romantic relationships.
- Lack of trust.
- Extreme mood swings.

Disorganized Attachment in Adult Relationships

People with disorganized attachment can struggle in their relationships. Their contradictory behavior of wanting to belong, falling in love, and pushing others away to protect themselves from pain can confuse their partners.

These individuals are taught early on that their loved ones will hurt them. For this reason, they often reject closeness and affection. Being raised by unpredictable parents has probably taught you that you can't trust or depend on anyone. In relationships, you believe that disappointment, betrayal, and pain are inevitable.

Disorganized attachment can manifest itself in relationships in several ways.

Difficulty Being Themselves

People with disorganized attachment struggle to open up to their partners and discuss their deepest feelings. They keep their vulnerable side hidden from the world.

Those with disorganized attachment struggle to communicate with their partners.
https://www.pexels.com/photo/woman-and-man-sitting-on-brown-wooden-bench-984949/

Your loved ones often feel they don't know you since you prefer to keep everyone at a distance. Why get close to people if they will either hurt or abandon you?

Since people with disorganized attachment have a negative self-image, they may feel that others will judge or dislike them if they reveal their true selves to them.

Acting out

Disorganized attachers live in fear that everyone will abandon them. Their prophecy tends to come true as a result of their unpredictable behavior. They are usually difficult and distrustful in relationships, and their partners often find their actions intolerable.

You can lash out at your partner or become distant at the smallest disagreement or misunderstanding. Or you may not believe their love for you is genuine, which can frustrate them.

Eventually, your actions push your partner away. Unfortunately, you don't realize your role in ruining your relationships and continue in the negative and destructive pattern.

Pattern of Unhealthy Relationships

Disorganized attachers are usually stuck in an unhealthy loop. They subconsciously recreate their childhood trauma and end up with abusive, toxic, and fearful partners. When they get hurt or cheated on, this confirms their belief that people are untrustworthy.

Trust Issues

Living in an unhealthy cycle that started with abusive parents, then toxic partners, and self-sabotaging behavior has taught you that you can't trust anyone. You believe that you can't rely on the people in your life or let them in because no one will ever love and accept you. This belief can drive you to jealousy and suspicious behavior.

For instance, you may think that your partner is cheating on you, so you demand they constantly tell you their whereabouts. No matter what they do or say, you still don't believe them. The lack of trust eventually drives your partner away.

Difficulty Regulating Emotions

People with disorganized attachment have difficulty regulating their emotions and are prone to anger and mood swings. This can lead to constant conflicts with your partner. For instance, your partner travels for work and is very excited about this trip because it will further their career.

Instead of showing your support and being happy for them, you get angry because they didn't ask you to come along. You start yelling at them and crying, believing that they will abandon you.

This leaves your partner bewildered as they don't understand the reason behind your behavior. Perhaps if you open up to them about your childhood and abandonment issues, they will be more understanding.

Demanding Behavior

Disorganized attachers can be demanding and clingy in relationships. They may exhibit unfavorable behaviors since they desperately crave their partner's attention, approval, and love.

For instance, you call your partner several times during the day just to check in, even if they are at work. You also insist on going with them when they are out with friends or visiting family. This leaves your partner feeling suffocated.

You also overanalyze everything they do or say due to your fear of abandonment.

Avoidant Behavior

You expect your partner to neglect your needs like your parents did. So, you keep an emotional distance from them and can come off as insensitive and cold in relationships. You refrain from expressing your feelings towards them. You can act aloof when they talk about the future or how much they love you.

Inconsistent Behavior

Your contradictory behavior of desiring and avoiding emotional closeness can make you seem hot and cold. One moment, you tell your partner you love them, and the other, you yell at them to leave you. Or you can be chatty and warm one day, and suddenly, you become withdrawn.

These mixed signals can be very confusing. The constant up and down can damage your partner's mental health. They may leave you just to protect themselves.

Without realizing it, disorganized attachers can become abusers and hurt the people who love them.

Sabotaging Relationships

You go into relationships with one foot out the door. You believe that your partner will either leave you or cheat on you, so you push them away or end the relationship before they do.

Imagine someone adopting a puppy. The owner provides the puppy with shelter, food, and water. However, they treat him terribly. Although the puppy is always full and warm, it is constantly on edge and feels threatened. It doesn't know whether its unpredictable owner will yell at or pet it the next time they walk through the door.

One day, a loving family adopts the puppy and showers it with love and affection. However, the puppy is still wary of them, constantly on high alert, and keeps its distance from the new family. After everything it has seen, the puppy can't feel safe in its new environment.

This is similar to a disorganized detacher. No matter how much your partner loves you and makes you feel safe, you are on edge, expecting them to turn against you at any moment, just like your parents.

Case Study

Anna and Jason had a two-year-old son called Danny. Jason was a drug addict and physically, verbally, and emotionally abusive to Anna. Anna was also addicted to drugs and had mental issues as a result of her traumatic childhood.

Upon examination, it was discovered that Anna struggled with regulating her emotions and forming close and healthy relationships, which was clear from her choice of partner.

She often felt angry, afraid, ashamed, and insecure in all her relationships, whether with family, partners, or friends. She desired to be close and connect with others, but she was also afraid of intimacy.

Since Danny lived with his mother, he started to copy her behavior. He often withdrew from others and kept his distance from his friends. Although he wanted to bond with children his age, he displayed violent behavior, even when playing.

When medical professionals evaluated him, they realized that he had developmental issues, impulsive behavior, struggled with emotional regulation, and was unable to relate to children his age. His doctors believed that all his problems were linked to his frightening and unpredictable relationship with his mother.

It was clear that both the mother and child suffered from disorganized attachment. They couldn't form intimate emotional bonds with each other or anyone else.

Anna's attachment problems began in childhood. Her parents were physically abusive to each other, and she witnessed them on multiple occasions engaged in physical fights. Her father was an alcoholic, and his behavior terrified her as a child.

She also had memories of witnessing various family members engaging in sexual acts right in front of her. As a child, this was traumatizing. She also experienced rejection from everyone in her life, including her mother, therapist, teachers, and sister.

Feeling rejected by the people who were supposed to love and support her destroyed her self-esteem.

Anna's chaotic childhood impacted her adult relationships. She ended up with Jason, who was violent and abusive like her father. Anna recreated with him the same toxic dynamic her parents had with each other.

Although Anna knew the impact Jason's violence had on Danny, she couldn't leave him. Jason was the most intimate relationship she ever had. He temporarily made Anna feel less empty because she experienced intense emotions that made her feel alive. Albeit, these emotions were negative and toxic, and she was addicted to them like a drug.

Deep down, Anna wanted to protect Danny, but the thought of leaving what she had with Jason terrified her.

When Danny started treatment, he was hyperactive, aggressive, and unable to speak. Although he was violent and often hit other children, his actions weren't out of aggression or anger. It was the only way he learned to connect with others.

During treatment, doctors started to impose some limitations on Danny to see how he would react. He often became angry, threw tantrums, and bit others. When he felt overwhelmed, he put his finger in his mouth and made himself vomit. Vomiting became an unhealthy coping strategy that he did at least once a day. After a couple of weeks, he didn't even need to put his finger in his mouth and automatically threw up when upset.

Treatment wasn't easy on Anna, who was struggling with regulating her emotions and being there for Danny. However, this proved to be a bonding experience for the mother and child. Anna related to Danny's emotions and behavior and tried to give him the love and support she never had.

Anna admitted to her doctors that she threw up to cope with overwhelming emotions. She believed that Danny saw her do it a couple of times and was only copying her behavior.

Anna and Danny were both struggling to regulate their emotions. Anna wanted to support and comfort her son but found his behavior triggering. Most parents can respond to their child acting out right away. However, parents with disorganized attachment are triggered by their child's behavior and are left stuck dealing with memories of their childhood trauma.

Anna tried to connect with her son during this challenging time. However, her anxiety and trauma made her a frightening figure rather than a comforting one. Danny wanted to be near his mother, but her unpredictable behavior scared him. He got close to her and then withdrew, which Anna misinterpreted as rejection. This contradiction in his emotions was a clear sign of disorganized attachment.

Anna didn't want her son to grow up with the same emotional baggage as her. She tried to be affectionate and supportive, but Danny was violent and aggressive, and Anna found her son's behavior challenging. Whenever she tried to hug him and calm him down, he would resort to biting, vomiting, and kicking. Anna couldn't tolerate his actions and either got angry or withdrew from him.

Anna and Danny attended a group attachment intervention. Anna was very engaged and friendly, but Danny acted out and was very aggressive. She tried to be there for her son, but she was concerned that the doctors and other parents might judge her parenting skills. She also wasn't sure how to respond to his emotional needs.

The therapists urged Anna to observe her son while he played and provided her with guidance and feedback. She was eager to learn and be the parent she never had. She followed their advice and often asked questions about how to approach him.

However, Anna was occasionally overwhelmed by her anxiety and dissociated from her son.

The therapists didn't give up on the mother and child. They approached Danny to play with him and invited Anna to join them. She could connect her son's play with his emotional state. She noticed that he started to feel calmer when he played with giraffes instead of lions and was excited to engage with his mother and doctor. Although he couldn't speak, he would just hand them the toys and make noises while playing.

Therapists taught Anna how to respond to her son when he was angry and aggressive. Seeing other adults accept Danny and treat him affectionately made her feel accepted. When the therapist calmed him down, Anna believed for the first time that it was possible to teach her son to regulate his emotions.

Anna's anxiety and fear of judgment didn't go away. She felt uncomfortable attending group therapy, and she and Danny stopped attending sessions. One of the therapists suggested private therapy sessions, and Anna was very excited about the idea.

In the comfort of a one-on-one session, Anna opened up about her abusive childhood and how these feelings didn't go away. Anna spoke of her mother's cold behavior and how she preferred her sister over her. Although she was angry with her parents, she felt protective of them. Anna also explored her relationship with Jason and how it wasn't a safe environment for Danny.

The more Anna trusted her therapists, the more vulnerable she became. Eventually, Anna found the courage to break up with Jason finally. Although it was hard, letting go of the toxic pattern was necessary.

Anna attended therapy with her son for over a year. It was a long and hard road, but she learned to cope with her traumatic childhood and be a good parent to Danny. The young boy became calmer and learned healthy coping mechanisms to deal with his pain.

Anna, who became more confident in herself and her son, returned to group therapy to continue their recovery.

Exercise 1: Journaling

Reflect on your life and write down any memories or current experiences that you believe are associated with disorganized attachment.

_____

_____

_____

Exercise 2: Mindful Meditation

Mindful Meditation is a great way to detach and really focus on your thoughts to organize them.

https://www.pexels.com/photo/woman-in-black-top-sitting-on-brown-armchair-3331574/

Instructions:

1. Find a quiet room away from distractions.

2. Sit in an upright and comfortable position and close your eyes.

3. Plant your feet firmly on the ground, and place both hands in your lap.

4. Breathe in and out through your nostrils.

5. Your breaths should be long and deep.

6. Tune out the world and only focus on your breathing.

7. Different thoughts may creep in interrupting your meditation.

8. Acknowledge them without judgment.

9. If they stirred certain emotions, mention how you feel aloud without judgment by saying "anger" or "fear."

10. Once you acknowledge the thoughts and emotions, let them go and refocus on your breathing.

11. Remain in this state for 15 to 20 minutes.

12. Treat distracting thoughts the same way you did in the previous steps.

You aren't responsible for your traumatic childhood. No child chooses their parents or environment. However, you now know better and can make choices to heal and grow. You have taken a big step, but the road is still long. Head to the next chapter to learn how childhood shapes your attachment.

Section 2: How Childhood Shapes Attachment

Young Billy was a terror in his childhood, but his grandmother loved him more than anything. The granny, aged 64, was fond of watching her little Spider-Man play and whoosh around. The older woman doted on Billy so much that his mother had no issues leaving him with her more often than not.

Billy learned to seek solace in his grandmother's arms, solace he wished he could get from his mother. He was raised by his single mother, who struggled with her own demons. She always confused him with a burst of attention for a while and then nothing. Sometimes, he wondered if he'd done something to make her mad.

He's usually excited and scared at the same time about the moment she comes to pick him up from his granny's. Billy loved his mom, but he couldn't help wondering which version of his mom he would be going home with every time he got in the passenger seat. He went with her anyway. She is his mom, after all, and who knows, maybe that's how all moms are. Decades later, the little boy grew to become one of the many people with a disorganized attachment style.

The truth is that seeds of attachment are sown deep within the fertile soil of a child's heart. The seeds grow into a forest, and you cannot fully separate the two. The idea of children screams attachment like a yellow flower amid dark and broody flowers. The child is designed to depend on their primary caregiver for everything. As fun as it might have been to watch, little Billy has no business with the kitchen in the name of cooking.

Your step toward healing is acknowledged. You're doing great. Don't lose hope; you're on the right track. Step further into the chapter and explore the fundamentals of forming attachment styles during childhood; all you need to know. Activities and fun exercises are scattered across this chapter to help you make sense of everything even more.

The source of attachment styles stems from childhood experiences.

Fundamental Principles of Attachment Styles

You must have passed by the profiles of the different attachment styles, avoidant, anxious, and disorganized, on your way to this section. You can flip back for reference if you have to. At this point, you probably have your behaviors under scrutiny, scanning for where people like you fall in. You may indeed have a disorganized attachment style, or it could be any of the other two. These attachment styles help people understand why they feel so close to some people and not others, hanging the sun right over the things that make people act the way they do in relationships with one another.

As children, how people bond with those caring for them, like their parents or guardians, shapes their bonding style with people around them as they grow and evolve. That's pretty much the way it is. How and why does this happen? Picture these scenarios while looking at some principles to help you understand it better:

Caregiver Response: When Evelyn was a baby, she naturally sought comfort and safety from her caregiver, her dad, Nathan. He was always so loving and gentle with her. He responded with love and care, regardless of whether she was a good girl, so Evelyn felt safe. It came naturally. She knew Daddy would catch her if he threw her up in the air. There was nothing that could convince her otherwise. The little girl loved her dad. The feeling built up into a "secure attachment," where Evelyn trusted that Daddy would always be there for her. This type of attachment is a healthy and positive bond between a child and their primary caregiver.

Consistent Caregiver: The caregiver feeds, comforts, and plays with you regularly. The consistency of their actions makes you feel safe and taken care of. For instance, though he loved her, Evelyn's father struggled to maintain consistency in their daily routine. He sometimes prepared delicious meals for Evelyn, read her bedtime stories, and played with her. On other days, however, he had to work late or was too tired to engage with Evelyn as much as he would have liked. This inconsistency started to affect Evelyn. Sometimes, she would act out, seeking attention from her father in any way she could. Other times, she would retreat into herself, feeling sad and lonely. If the primary caregiver is sometimes there and sometimes not, it can make someone feel unsure and anxious. This inconsistency can lead to an "insecure attachment."

Emotional Connection: When caregivers understand how the children under their care feel and show that they care, it helps the children build strong relationships with them. Take a look at Evelyn and her father again. Evelyn's dad was always there for her, listening to and comforting her when she was upset. He would hug her tightly and reassure her that everything would be okay. This made Evelyn feel safe and loved. She knew she could always turn to her father when she needed support. The man had also taught Evelyn that expressing her emotions is okay. He would encourage her to talk about her feelings and validate her emotions, letting her know it was normal to feel that way. This helped Evelyn learn to identify and express her feelings healthily. She developed a strong bond with her father because of his emotional availability and support.

Learning from Caregivers: Learning about relationships is a big part of growing up. Most people don't even know that it's a thing. Relationships are like mirrors. We learn a lot from our caregivers and tend to reflect their values. They teach us how to love, trust, and respect others based on how they treat us. Evelyn's dad always showed her love, trust, and respect. Nathan listened to her when she talked and treated her with kindness and understanding. Evelyn learned from there that relationships should be based on love and mutual respect.

However, if caregivers are not loving or respectful, children may develop negative beliefs about relationships. For example, if a child grows up seeing their parents fight all the time, they might think that's how all relationships should be. But when children see love, trust, and respect in their caregivers, they're more likely to develop positive beliefs about relationships themselves.

Cultural and Environmental Factors: Cultural norms, family traditions, and community values influence how caregivers interact with their children. For Evelyn and her daddy, growing up in a community that valued family greatly influenced their relationship. Nathan's parents and grandparents had strong family traditions and cultural beliefs, and that shaped his attentive and affectionate parenting style. This nurturing environment strengthened the father-daughter bond. However, children who have some traumatic experiences or are victims of family disruptions will most likely end up developing feelings of insecurity and fear of abandonment.

Childhood Trauma Influences How We Bond with Others

Evelyn loved spending evenings curled up beside her dad, Nathan, listening to his stories. They were a team, just the two of them, ever since Evelyn's mom passed away when she was just a tiny tot. Nathan, a single father, juggled work and home life with everything he had, showering Evelyn with love and doing his best to fill the void left by her mother's absence.

One sunny afternoon, everything changed. While playing with friends, Evelyn overheard a hushed conversation between adults. Granddaddy was "gone." The man who usually kept a Snickers bar in his pockets for her. The girl couldn't believe it. Once filled with sunshine and laughter, her world suddenly turned dark and scary. The playful evenings of storytelling with her dad became filled with Evelyn's tearful questions and Nathan's choked sobs. He tried his best to comfort her, but his grief mirrored hers, leaving them both feeling lost and alone.

The loss of her grandfather, the one constant male figure in her life besides her father, hit the little girl hard. She became withdrawn, clinging to her dad like a life raft. She started having nightmares, waking up in the middle of the night, desperately searching for her dad. Nathan, overwhelmed by grief and the responsibility of comforting his daughter, found it difficult to offer the consistent, patient support the poor girl needed.

This traumatic experience, coupled with how her mother is nowhere to be found, affected the natural development of Evelyn's attachment patterns. She struggled to trust, fearing another painful loss. Her once playful spirit dimmed, replaced by a constant sense of anxiety and a fear of being abandoned.

Following the trauma, she now exhibits behaviors associated with disorganized attachment. For example, she shows conflicting behaviors, such as seeking comfort from her father but then pushing him away when he tries to console her. The unpredictability and confusion in seeking and avoiding closeness are typical of disorganized attachment.

Nathan's struggle to respond to Evelyn's needs consistently and supportively can further contribute to her disorganized attachment style, as she may not know how to interpret her father's responses or rely on him for comfort. Traumatic experiences during childhood can significantly impact attachment styles. It ends up summoning the disorganized attachment, characterized by fear, confusion, and unresolved emotions.

Effects of Separation During Childhood on Attachment Style

Five-year-old Ben, a bundle of boundless energy and infectious laughter, loved spending time with each of his parents. They were his whole world, a happy family, but things changed. Amid the warmth and joy, a storm brewed. His parents had problems, facing challenges they couldn't overcome, and soon enough, they decided to separate.

This really upset little Ben a lot. He felt confused and scared because he loved them both. It was hard for him to understand why they couldn't stay together. Why couldn't they just kiss and make up like they do in the movies? As the news of their separation sank in, Ben's world bent to one side. The once-familiar walls of his home started to feel unfamiliar, charged with a tension almost visible.

The separation was a major blow to Ben's developing sense of security. He felt torn between his mom and dad, wishing to the stars that his family would be whole again, even if it felt like a distant dream. The confusion and uncertainty left him questioning his family's future and the basis of love and trust.

As Ben grew older, the impact of this early separation continued to ripple outwards, affecting how he formed relationships. He found it difficult to fully open up to others; a constant wariness resided within. The fear of abandonment, a constant shadow cast by his childhood experience, kept him guarded, making it challenging to build deep and secure connections. Intimacy felt risky, a potential gateway to another heartbreak. He didn't like it the first time. He had no intention of experiencing that again.

The good news is no matter how small, Ben, as stubborn as he has always been, had a spark of hope. Something that had the potential of torching a whole forest zone down. He understood that his past experiences, while impactful, didn't define his future. He embarked on a personal journey of self-discovery, seeking to understand his emotions and attachment patterns. He began to work on healing his childhood wounds, learning to trust himself and others, and gradually chipping away at the walls she had built around his heart.

Like many others, Ben's story highlights the lasting impact of early experiences on attachment development. The little boy's evolution into a man is a testament to the human spirit's ability to heal, grow, and seek the connections that nourish the soul, even after adversity.

Case Study

Lena is a woman in her thirties who has faced many challenges due to her disorganized attachment style. Her childhood was marked by significant trauma, including physical abuse and neglect. Her mother, her primary caregiver, was frequently emotionally unavailable and inconsistent in her care. Their relationship was a hot and cold dance.

These early experiences left Lena with deep fears and emotional struggles. As a result, she developed a disorganized attachment style. In her adult relationships, Lena finds it incredibly challenging to trust others. She often pushes people away when they try to get close to her, fearing they will abandon her, just like her mother did.

She struggles with intimacy and trust affects her ability to form healthy, lasting relationships. She yearns for connection but is plagued by the fear of being hurt again. This fear often leads her to sabotage her relationships, creating a self-fulfilling prophecy of abandonment.

Despite these challenges, Lena stays strong-headed, never giving up. She is actively seeking help and support to overcome her attachment issues. She is slowly learning to trust others and form healthier relationships through therapy and self-reflection. She is beginning to understand that her past does not define her future and that she deserves love and companionship.

Lena's story is a reminder of the lasting impact of childhood experiences on adult relationships. Don't be scared to seek help and support to heal from past traumas and develop secure attachments. If Lena could break out, so can you. Take your experiences into your own hands and make of them what you'll. You are in charge of your life. Act like it!

Activity 1: Guided Visualization

Guided Visualization helps you delve deeper into your childhood and address buried issues.

https://www.pexels.com/photo/woman-and-man-doing-yoga-pose-on-mountain-area-6298342/

Step 1: Close your eyes and take a deep breath. Imagine yourself as a child, back in your childhood home. Picture the rooms, the furniture, and the familiar surroundings. Remember a specific memory from your early childhood, perhaps a moment with your mom or dad that stands out to you. Maybe it was in your backyard or a corner in the living room. Feel the air on your skin, smell familiar scents, and let your ears hear the sounds associated with that place in your memory.

Step 2: Reminisce on how you felt during that memory. Did you feel safe and loved, or were you scared and unsure? Consider how your caregiver responded to your emotions. How did they interact with you? Were they comforting and understanding, or did they seem distant or unresponsive? Did they show you love and affection? Pay attention to how these interactions, or lack of, made you feel.

Step 3: Consider how this memory may have influenced your attachment style. If you felt safe and loved, you may have developed a secure attachment style, where you feel comfortable depending on others and expressing your emotions. If you felt scared or unsure, you may have developed an insecure attachment style, where you struggle with trust and intimacy.

Step 4: Step outside your memory now; take a moment to reflect on how these early experiences have shaped your relationships and attachment style today. What emotions come up when you think about your childhood experiences? Are there any patterns you can find in how your caregiver interacted with you? Now that you can see the bigger picture, consider how you can use this awareness to build healthy relationships and connections with good people in the future.

Step 5: When you're ready, slowly open your eyes and return to the present moment. Take a few breaths and reflect on the emotions or insight that you experienced. If any memories or emotions become too overwhelming, don't hesitate. Quickly redirect your focus and seek professional help.

Reflective Writing Exercise:

Take a moment to list at least five qualities and behaviors of your early caregivers and how they affected you. How did they express love, show affection, and provide support? Consider whether they were consistent in their care, responsive to your needs, and emotionally available.

1._____

_____

2. _____

_____

3. _____

_____

4. _____

_____

5. _____

_____

Reflect on how these qualities may have impacted your current relationship patterns and attachment style. For example, if your caregivers were loving and supportive, you may have developed a secure attachment style, feeling comfortable with intimacy and trust in your relationships. But if your caregivers were distant or inconsistent, you may have developed an insecure attachment style.

Discussion Questions

These questions are meant to spark conversations within yourself, with friends, or even in support groups. Remember, there are no right or wrong answers, just honest reflections and shared experiences.

- Did anything in this chapter resonate with you? Maybe you recognized certain patterns in your own relationships or had "a-ha" moments about your childhood. Share your stories and see if others have similar experiences.

- Have you noticed any challenges in your current relationships that may be linked to your attachment style? How do you navigate these challenges?

- What strategies have you found helpful in cultivating healthier relationship attachment patterns? Have you sought professional help or support in this process?

- How do you think cultural and environmental factors have influenced your attachment style? Are any specific cultural norms or traditions shaping your views on relationships?

- In what ways do you think your attachment style has evolved or changed over time? What events or experiences do you think have influenced these changes?

- How do you approach forming attachments with others? Do you find it easy to trust and depend on others, or do you struggle with intimacy and closeness?

- Have you ever considered how your attachment style may impact your parenting or caregiving style? How do you strive to create a secure attachment with your own children or loved ones?

- What insights or discoveries have you made about yourself through exploring your attachment style? How has this understanding influenced your relationships and self-awareness?

- What are your hopes for building healthier relationships in the future? Knowing your goals can be a powerful motivator. Share your aspirations and inspire others to work towards their own fulfilling connections.

Section 3: Recognizing and Overcoming Unhealthy Patterns

The only way to turn your life around and begin building healthier attachments in relationships is to identify the unhealthy ones. To help you get started, this chapter will guide you through the challenging journey of revealing and altering maladaptive behaviors, which are the hallmarks of disorganized attachment. Reading it, you'll learn about the common characteristics of harmful attachment patterns and how to identify these, when sorting through your own experiences.

Once you learn what to look for, the second part of the chapter will help you take the crucial first step toward healthier relationships — recognizing unhealthy patterns. It focuses on reflection and engagement exercises that promote self-awareness, pinpoint specific areas for improvement in your relationships, and explore new ways of interacting that can break old patterns and lead to more positive outcomes.

We tend to react in irrational ways when we have unhealthy attachments; this is why we need to recognize patterns.

https://www.pexels.com/photo/a-man-and-a-woman-arguing-5616190/

The Common Characteristics Of Unhealthy Attachment Patterns

Unhealthy attachment patterns negatively impact relationships because they cause plenty of difficulties regardless of the nature of your connection. The problem is that they're incredibly insidious and invisible, almost imperceptible. You won't even know it's happening, and you'll fall into the trap of unhealthy attachment. And because you don't know it's happening, you're continuing the behavior, becoming part of a never-ending cycle. That is - *if* you don't take the proactive approach and decide to look into your current behavioral patterns in your relationships and how your past experience may influence these.

You see, as bad your attachment style may be, it's not set in stone. You can change. However, first, you must learn what you're working with.

Uncovering and altering maladaptive parchment patterns requires intentional effort — and a little help from the subsection enlisting the common characteristics of these behaviors below.

Thinking the Other Person Is Ignoring You

Do you tend to think the person is thinking something bad about you or is doing something that may hurt you when they don't respond to you immediately? People with unhealthy attachment patterns expect others to be instantly available as soon as they send a message or call them.

In reality, people have busy lives and don't have the time to hang on to their phones waiting for someone's text or call. So, if this is something you identify with, consider that the other person is busy and will call/text back later instead of getting upset that they didn't do it right away and think they're ignoring you.

Putting Your Needs Aside

Not being bothered to fulfill your needs (because you're too busy trying to meet someone else's) is another surefire sign of unhealthy attachment. In the worst-case scenario, you'll push your needs so far to the back of your mind that you'll completely forget about them — at least consciously. Unmet needs can bubble up when their number increases, causing far more trouble for your life and well-being than if expressed immediately.

If you find yourself constantly focusing on the other person's needs, hoping to meet their requirements, reflecting on your own needs is a good idea. Sometimes, you'll be so focused on fulfilling the other person's desires you don't even realize they don't want you to. So, by turning to your own needs from time to time, you'll be doing them a favor.

False Expectations of Happiness

Those with unhealthy attachment patterns want relationships because they think this is the only way to find happiness. They don't know how to cultivate joy and happiness from the inside, so they outsource it. For example, in romantic relationships, a person will seek a partner with the expectation that they'll be their soulmate. While the partner may contribute to their happiness, they will only gratify their unfulfilled need for a connection.

Remember, the first person to look for happiness is you. Only you know that can bring you joy and fulfillment. Relying on another person to make you happy will do anything but.

Thinking You Can't Have a Future Without Them

Similarly to the false expectations of happiness, you might think you can't imagine not having the other person in your life. Whether you just met this person or have known them for years, you believe having a future without them is impossible. Or if this future is possible, it's looking very bleak.

As hard as it is to imagine your future without them, the only way to break from this mindset is to do exactly that. Would you truly not survive without them in your life?

Constantly Seeking Approval

People with unhealthy attachment styles fail to prioritize their own needs and become preoccupied with meeting the other person's needs because they constantly seek external validation. They become people-pleasers by looking for this person's approval. They cannot do anything without checking it with this person, fearing they might disapprove of it.

Moreover, the constant need for approval can be even detrimental to a person's mental health. Worrying about what the other person thinks can lead to depression and anxiety.

Motivation to fulfill other people's needs is rooted in a lack of self-love and self-confidence. If you've recognized this pattern in your relationship(s), know that boosting your self-confidence is the best way to find reassurance in your abilities.

Avoiding Emotional Intimacy

Unhealthy attachment patterns can also lead to the person wanting to avoid emotional intimacy. No one likes to feel vulnerable, but if you feel that you can't even open up emotionally in your closest relationships, you need to explore why. The healthiest and strongest relationships are built on trust, which can only be cultivated when the parties are unafraid to be vulnerable in front of each other. If you can't do this but the other person wants to, they'll feel pushed away.

If you find cultivating emotional intimacy overwhelming, working on self-regulation and using some self-soothing techniques can help overcome the obstacles.

Lack of Trust

Being hyper-focused on the other person's needs, thoughts, emotions, and behavior can easily lead to a lack of trust. After all, if you spend all that time scrutinizing their every move, you are bound to find something that'll make you believe you can't trust them. One of the telltale signs of this lack of trust is excessive jealousy.

Instead of becoming obsessed over the other person's moves, why not focus on your growth and development? It will boost your self-esteem and chase away your insecurities, and you won't have time to think about whether you can trust them.

Tendency to Jump to Conclusions

Poor self-regulatory skills, lack of trust, and having primary unfulfilled needs are dangerous combinations with a disorganized attachment style. They can make you jump to conclusions about the other person's motive or actions. Since this judgment will likely be negative, it will trigger hurtful emotions. If you can't control these, you'll act even without having a single piece of evidence that would confirm the thought process that leads to that conclusion.

Developing a habit of stopping and considering whether the negative feelings or thoughts about the other person are valid will go a long way toward learning not to act on your emotions.

Not Prioritizing Alone Time

Do you spend most of your time with the other person? Or take time for yourself, too? Having alone time is crucial for self-care. Unfortunately, unhealthy attachment makes people so focused on the other person that they can never be alone. Even if they can, they don't know what to do with themselves or feel it's "too quiet" without the other person being around.

You'll understand how valuable alone time is when you integrate it into your routine.
Photo by Jure Širić: https://www.pexels.com/photo/woman-wearing-black-long-sleeved-shirt-sitting-on-green-grass-field-691919/

Obsessing Over the Other Person's Interests

Beyond becoming hyperfocused on the other person's needs and wants, those with ill attachment styles can also see the other person's goals and aspirations as theirs and experience their successes as their own.

By putting aside your own aspirations and interests, you are living someone else's life, which can never be as fulfilling as living yours could be. Be authentic and seek your own interests if you want to overcome unhealthy attachment patterns.

Thinking You Need to Rescue Them

Being the first person your loved one thinks of in times of need may seem reassuring, but wanting to rescue them all the time is unhealthy. It's a way of controlling someone's life, which can cause a divide in your relationship.

Challenges are part of life, and everyone must learn how to navigate them by themselves. If they seek your assistance, feel free to offer a helping hand, but if they don't, let them resolve their issues on their own.

The need to control the other person can go way beyond wanting to help them through tough times. It can lead you to meddle in the most trivial things, like what they wear for a job interview. You might think that you're doing them a favor (and even have the best intentions) by forcing them to wear a shirt that, in your eyes, makes them look more professional. However, this won't guarantee their success — and if they don't like the shirt, it can make them feel uncomfortable and insecure, which further lowers their chances of acing the interview.

The Need for Constant Reassurance

Those with attachment issues often feel about the feelings of their loved ones for them. This also stems from low self-esteem and insecurities, like the constant need for approval. Wanting to feel your partner tells you they love you all the time is the perfect example of seeking reassurance in a relationship.

Have you ever considered that there are several ways to show love? Verbally expressing it isn't the only way. Some people prefer showing it through actions. Reflecting on how the other person expresses their love and care for you can help reassure you of their feelings.

Feeling Like Your Feelings Aren't Reciprocated

You might wish to hear the other person cares for you just as much as you care for them. Otherwise, you can start thinking that your feelings aren't reciprocated. Wandering whether this is true or why they can't feel for you as intensely as you feel for them can lead to even more insecurities and mental health issues.

In most cases, your suspicions will be unfounded, and the person will care for you just as you do for them. If they don't, exploring their feelings and yours is the only way to know this.

Sensing Something Is Wrong

If you sense something is off about your relationship but can't pinpoint what's wrong, it may be because of a disorganized attachment. With unhealthy attachment styles, even being happy can become overwhelming, especially in intimate relationships. The other person's closeness will intensify all your feelings about them, including your need to please, help, and be reassured by them.

Like in the previous example, there might be nothing untoward going on, but you'll feel like it is because your previous experiences led to unhealthy beliefs about relationships.

Uncertainty about the Relationship

You might also feel that your relationship has no future. You might think you'll never be able to please them enough (as much as you try) or make them feel like you do, so they'll inevitably end your relationship.

Engaging them in building a "we" mindset can teach you that they'll always be honest about their feelings. If they want to end the relationship, they'll tell you so you don't have to wonder — and if they don't, you can save yourself from all that worry over whether your relationship has a future.

Failing to Set and Respect Boundaries

Setting healthy boundaries is the foundation of building a healthy relationship. If you have attachment issues, failing to do so will only make it easier for you to put aside your needs. Your loved ones can't respect the line you haven't even drawn.

In the same vein, if you don't have boundaries for others to worry about, this may make you think your loved ones don't have them either. If you're unfamiliar with the concept of healthy boundaries, you may even fail to understand why someone would get offended by you disrespecting their limits.

Becoming hyper-focused on their needs, wanting to control and rescue them, and pushing for reassurance all the time are examples of not considering the other person's boundaries.

Setting your own limits will teach you the importance of these emotional skills in your and your loved ones' lives.

Fear of Abandonment

Do you fear that a loved one will abandon you one day? If yes, this can even intensify your need for reassurance and approval. Fear of abandonment is a challenging emotion to overcome because it's often rooted in traumatic childhood experiences of being or feeling abandoned by someone. For starters, consider whether you have a valid reason for this fear.

Constant Need for Communication

This goes hand in hand with control. Healthy communication is necessary for a relationship, but bad emotional attachment styles can easily make you cross the line. As mentioned before, your loved one probably has a busy life, and they can't communicate everything to you in real time. You can't expect them to be around or on call with you all day.

Instead of focusing on the quantity of your communication, turn your attention to its quality. What the other person conveys to you in communication is infinitely more important than how frequently you talk throughout the day.

Emotional Overdependence

Ever noticed your mood changing wherever you are around a certain person? While it's okay to be sad when you can't talk or have a conflict with them, letting your emotions depend on what the other person says or does isn't healthy. If this person doesn't validate your feelings or actions as you require them to, your mood is ruined for the rest of the day. The best way to combat this is to explore what triggers your emotions.

Frequent Crying Spells

A somewhat overt but all the more common sign of emotional dependence brought on by unhealthy attachment is getting teary-eyed about everything that has to do with the other person.

If you're easily prone to crying at these things, exploring why they have such a massive emotional hold on you can be a good way to stop the waterworks.

Compromising On Your Values

Since people with unhealthy attachment styles center their lives around those they're in a relationship with, this can lead them to compromise their morals and beliefs. There is nothing wrong with having shared values and morals in a relationship. However, letting the other person take over can harm your health and happiness. On the other hand, working on personal growth is a superb way of bringing your values back to focus.

Feelings Possessive Over the Other Person

Thinking that no one can please the other person as you do is another hallmark of unhealthy attachment patterns. This unhealthy possessiveness can hinder the development of your relationship, so it's best to end it by disabusing yourself of the notion that you should be the most important person in your loved one's life.

Being Resentful

Another way to hurt your relationship is to play games, which can lead to a lot of hurt feelings. Eventually, they'll start resenting you, and you'll start resenting them, making both of you deeply unhappy. Stop trying to manipulate the other person to prevent this mutual resentment from taking root.

The Need to Have Your Feelings Controlled By the Other Person

Beyond compromising one's values and needs, unhealthy attachment can also lead one to allow others to control their feelings. If you ever change your feelings because the person you're in a relationship with convinced you to do so, you've begun to sacrifice your beliefs and emotional needs. Exploring why this happened can help you combat the effects.

Letting Go Is Impossible

If you think a future without the other person doesn't exist and they're the only way to feel complete, the thought of letting go of the relationship can be paralyzing. Reflecting on your relationship dynamic is a helpful way to determine whether it's time to let go. Moreover, finding reasons why it doesn't work may help you see why you should make this step.

Self-Reflection Exercises for Uncovering Unhealthy Patterns

Active participation through self-reflection is crucial for uncovering unhealthy attachment patterns. The following activities incorporate both, helping you become fully engaged in overturning your relationships.

Daily Relationship Diary

The best way to explore your relationship patterns is to maintain written records. By keeping a daily relationship diary, you can track the moments in your relationship that trigger emotional responses. As you make the entries, you can reflect on them and try to identify specific recurring patterns. This will help you develop a profound understanding of your needs, emotions, and values, bring awareness to problematic areas, and give you a starting place for improvement.

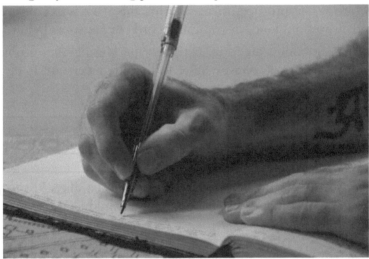

Commit to writing in your relationship diary on a daily basis to get a better understanding of what's going on.

When you sit down to make an entry, spend a few minutes sitting comfortably and letting your mind relax before picking up your pen. As you start writing about your daily experience, note when you felt bad about something related to your relationships. Consider the following points when reflecting on the experiences:

- What was the trigger that made you feel this way?
- Describe the worst part of the experience.

- Consider why the incident had this effect.
- Has anything similar happened before? If yes, did it have the same effect?

The insights you gain through your relationship diary will help you better understand your existing relationship and unhelpful triggers.

Role Playing Exercise

Through this exercise, you can write out or enact conversations that typically lead to conflict or discomfort in their relationships. When coming up with specific conversations where emotional responses arose, experiment with different responses or communication styles in these scenarios. This will help you explore new ways of interacting that can break old patterns and lead to more positive outcomes. Remember, changing deep-rooted behaviors can be challenging, but it is ultimately a one-step-at-a-time process.

Here are a few prompts to use during this exercise. You can read them and answer out loud, or you can record your answers below.

1. What emotions are you experiencing during the problematic situations? How do you convey these to the other person? Is there any way to better express them?

_____
_____
_____
_____

2. Do you try to avoid topics that may lead to conflicts just to please the other person? What would happen if you would let the conflict arise instead?

_____
_____
_____
_____

3. What do you need when trying to please the other person or avoid conflict with them? Is there any other way to obtain this?

_____
_____
_____
_____

4. When in your relationship do you expect perfection from yourself? Do you expect the same from the other person? If not, why?

_____

_____

_____

_____

5. How do you feel when you fail to be perfect? What do you do when you feel this way? Is there something more helpful you could do?

_____

_____

_____

_____

6. What words of kindness would you offer to yourself?

_____

_____

_____

_____

Section 4: The Path to Healing: Strategies for Emotional Repair

Healing is possible. It can be hard to imagine a life where you aren't attached to your past or ruled by your trauma. However, many people before you have found their way to recovery and you can, too. Before you begin this journey, you need to believe in yourself. Believe that you can move on from a past that no longer serves you or has any power over you.

There are a number of strategies that you can use to heal your wounds.
https://www.pexels.com/photo/white-pillar-candles-on-brown-woven-basket-6957386/

This section provides strategies and exercises to facilitate emotional healing.

Acknowledging and Accepting Your Wounds

Suppressed emotional wounds can appear in every area of your life and impact your interactions and behavior. The first step to heal and move on is to acknowledge and accept your trauma. This isn't always easy; for some, it can be a scary and painful step. However, it is necessary not just for you but for the people who care about you and want to see you get better.

Don't underestimate your need for emotional healing, or your mental health will suffer as a result. Instead of cultivating supportive and nurturing relationships, you'll find yourself in stressful and chaotic situations.

Emotional healing can mean something different for each person, depending on their trauma and experience. Whether it's going to therapy or cutting off your abusive caregiver, identify what you need to heal and take this step.

Accepting and acknowledging your emotional wounds can be a transforming experience.

Feeling Less Isolated

Ignoring your wounds can make you feel isolated. You may avoid places that trigger your pain or avoid socialization due to anxiety and depression that result from disorganized attachment. Isolation can negatively impact your mental health and your healing journey.

Acknowledging your wounds gives you a chance at a normal and happy life. When your past has no control over you, you'll be open to creating strong and meaningful relationships.

Dealing with Your Trauma

You may not realize the impact your trauma has on you until you self-reflect and acknowledge your pain. When you dig deep, you may find other underlying issues you didn't realize existed. This will allow you to confront and deal with these problems.

Improving Your Physical and Mental Health

Acknowledging and addressing your wounds can reduce stress, depression, and anxiety. Your emotional well-being and physical health are also connected. Confronting your pain can boost your immunity, reduce chronic pain, and improve your overall health.

Enhancing Your Emotional Intelligence

People develop emotional intelligence by recognizing their pain and learning to manage their emotions. Understanding your feelings teaches you to respond appropriately when negative emotions arise or when you are triggered.

This is one of the most significant skills one can have. It will help you make better decisions and easily navigate personal and professional relationships.

Increasing Your Resilience

Acknowledging emotional wounds can increase your resilience so you are better equipped to face adversity, handle stress, and overcome obstacles.

Promoting Personal Growth

Your trauma prevents you from growing, evolving, and reaching your full potential. Accepting and resolving your wounds will encourage you to live the life you have always wanted, follow your passions, and develop healthy coping mechanisms.

Nourishing Your Relationships

Addressing emotional issues can limit conflicts and misunderstandings in relationships. You will have the wisdom and mental clarity to communicate and have healthy conversations without being triggered.

Healing Your Pain

Burying your pain and pretending that it doesn't exist is easy. You may think that your wounds won't hurt you if you suppress them and avoid thinking about them. However, trauma has a way of resurfacing in the least expected moments. You can't avoid your pain; you can only confront it to heal. This can't happen without first acknowledging it.

The Power of Accepting Your Wounds

Everything you feel is here for a reason. You need your emotions to guide you to make the right decisions, steer you away from the wrong ones, and help you develop healthy relationships.

Dealing with your wounds requires you to first accept them as a part of your journey. Some people believe that accepting their past means surrendering to the pain and living with it. This isn't true. You don't have to hold on to painful memories or keep reliving the trauma.

Acceptance merely brings awareness to your wounds and allows you to embrace them while acknowledging they won't last.

Rather than struggling with your past or looking for ways to distract you from it, you learn to let go.

Accepting your wounds is realizing that your feelings will change one day. Even happiness doesn't last. No one is happy all the time. The same goes for negative emotions like sadness, anger, grief, defeat, etc.

Every emotion you will ever experience is temporary. Although you have been carrying your wounds for years, they won't be with you for the rest of your life. So accept them for what they are now and believe they are fleeting.

Healing from Your Emotional Wounds

After acknowledging and accepting your wounds, you can start the healing.

Take Small Steps

The path to healing can be long and challenging. Don't be in a hurry to get to the other side. Making many dramatic changes in a short time can be overwhelming, and you may not be able to commit to them.

Instead, make manageable, small changes that you can implement. This will give you a sense of accomplishment and motivate you to keep going.

Set Realistic Goals

Unrealistic goals that are impossible to achieve will leave you feeling frustrated. Why set goals that will disappoint you and lower your self-esteem? These feelings will only make you feel worse and affect your healing.

Before setting a goal, ask yourself whether you have the tools, skills, and time to achieve it. If you don't, make adjustments or find another objective. Don't waste your energy on something that you won't be able to achieve.

Your inability to achieve a goal doesn't make you a failure. Each person has their strengths and weaknesses. For instance, one person can face their abusive caregiver to get closure while the other can't.

Focus on what you can achieve. Remember, what matters is the journey, not the destination. You are learning something new every day and growing in different ways.

Be Patient with Yourself

You have been suffering from your emotional trauma for years, so don't expect to heal in a short period. Healing takes a lot of time, effort, and work. Be patient with yourself, and take your time to learn and gain new insights to evolve and grow.

One of the most common disappointments people face early on is believing their progress should remain consistent. Progress isn't a steady journey. Unfortunately, you aren't going to get better and better every day. It is more like two steps forward and one step backward.

You may face obstacles on the way. Some days, you'll be fine, while on others, everything will hit you like it happened. Don't give up when things get tough. Be persistent and understand that it is normal for challenges to arise.

Consider trying different approaches or challenging yourself. For instance, you join a support group but aren't getting any better. It has been months, and nothing has changed. Instead of feeling defeated and giving up, try a different approach like going to individual therapy.

Don't be hard on yourself. You are healing at your own pace. Keep your expectations realistic, be patient and persistent, and practice self-compassion. Accept that the path to healing may be longer and slower than you expect, and that's okay.

Learn from Every Obstacle

Setbacks are to be expected. Instead of feeling discouraged, view them as learning opportunities. You can learn more from your failures than successes as they will show you what doesn't work so you can evaluate your strategy and make the necessary adjustments.

Don't avoid setbacks; instead, welcome them as a part of your healing and be open to the lessons they will teach you.

Reflect on Your Past

Healing requires you to confront your feelings about the past. Trying to suppress them won't work. Negative emotions are stored in your unconscious mind and affect your thoughts, actions, and reactions. Ignoring them will only give them power over you.

For this reason, therapists always encourage their patients to feel their emotions. This step may be challenging as you may discover painful emotions you aren't ready to face.

Allow yourself to feel all your different emotions and express them in a healthy way. If you are sad, cry. If you are angry, talk to a friend. Release the pain.

You can try meditating and using the relaxation technique mentioned in the previous chapter to recognize your negative emotions, label them, and let them go without judgment. If you struggle with confronting these emotions, consider working with a therapist.

Refrain from Blame

Reflect on your trauma from a place of compassion and empathy rather than criticism, judgment, or blame. Just like disinfecting a physical wound, remove the bacteria from your emotional wounds. This bacteria is "blame."

Sometimes, when people think about their past, they can't help but blame those who hurt them, which can bring feelings of anger or resentment. Some people also blame themselves for putting up with the abuse, forgetting that they are the victims of their circumstances.

Blame is a dangerous game that will waste your time and energy and can damage your mental health. Refrain from blaming yourself or others and focus on forgiveness and self-compassion.

Practice Self-Care

Treat yourself with kindness and compassion. You'll burn out and feel drained if you ask a lot of yourself. Remember to save your energy because emotional healing can be exhausting.

Self-care is essential and often overlooked.
https://www.pexels.com/photo/woman-in-white-tank-top-lying-on-gray-bed-3673941/

Practice self-care by being attuned to your physical sensations, emotional needs, and mental health. Notice how you are feeling throughout the day. Are you calm or agitated? Are you happy or upset? Do you feel anxious? Do you have headaches? Are your muscles tense?

Your body and mind constantly tell you what they need, so listen and fulfill their needs. For instance, you have been working hard for the last few days and are exhausted. You can fulfill your body's needs by taking a few days off to travel, going to the spa, or just relaxing at home.

Let Go of the "All-or-Nothing" Mentality

If you expect that you have to completely heal for your life to get better, you are only prolonging your misery. Emotional repair doesn't happen right away or all at once. It will happen gradually and over time.

Any amount of healing, no matter how small, will positively impact your life. If you let go of the all-or-nothing mentality, you'll notice an improvement with every step you take on your path to recovery.

Although you haven't completely healed, you are in a better mood than you were a few months ago, have developed healthy coping mechanisms, and are learning to be more relaxed.

Do Things That Bring You Joy

Boost your mood by engaging in activities that bring you joy and help you relax and unwind. What are your hobbies? What do you like to do to refresh your mind? This can be activities like dancing, singing, painting, meditation, writing, or playing an instrument.

Incorporate these activities into your self-care routine. Treat them as a priority, and make time for them every day. For instance, you can schedule a few minutes before bed or after you wake up to meditate, paint, or write in your journal.

They can also be a form of self-expression. For instance, if you can't express your pain with words, you can paint what you are feeling.

Spending time doing things you enjoy will fill you with positive energy so you can deal with your wounds with a fresh perspective.

Choose Forgiveness

Forgiveness sets you free. Many people find this step hard because they can't forget what they have been through. Others feel that the person who hurts them doesn't deserve this kindness.

Understand that forgiveness has nothing to do with the other person. You forgive to set yourself free from anger, grudges, and pain. You let go of emotions that no longer serve you. The other person doesn't factor in this scenario.

It's okay if you can't forget. Some pain can be too strong to pretend that it has never happened. You can still forgive without forgetting what they did to you.

Forgiveness doesn't mean letting the abuser back into your life. You can let go and move on without seeing or speaking to them again.

Let go of the hate and resentment; these only tie you to the abuser. Forgive them so they no longer have power over you.

Seek Help

You don't have to travel this road alone. Understandably, asking for help isn't easy, especially if no one took care of your emotional needs as a child. However, since you are growing and healing, you can try opening yourself up to someone and asking for help.

Seeking help can provide you with emotional support and guidance. When you talk to someone you trust, they will make you feel accepted, which can have a huge impact on your self-esteem and mental health.

Talk to a friend, family member, or therapist, or join a support group. Surround yourself with positive people who are willing to help you get better.

Now that you understand the power of healing and have familiarized yourself with strategies to put you on the right path, you are ready for the practical part to apply everything you learned.

Exercise 1: Emotional Mapping

Use the template below and create an emotional map, tracing back to specific events or experiences related to your attachment issues. For instance, think of a moment that made you angry. What other anger-related emotions did you experience at that moment? Did you feel resentful, upset, furious, etc.? Write what you felt under the anger category.

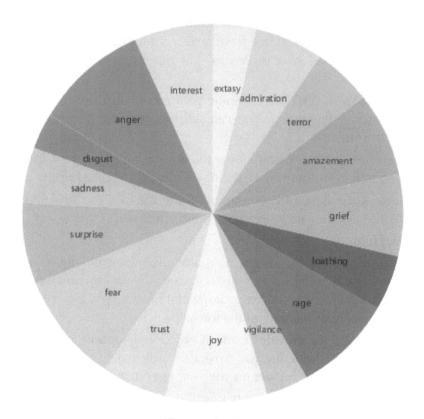

Your emotional map.
Attribution-ShareAlike 2.0 Generic, CC BY-SA 2.0 DEED
<https://creativecommons.org/licenses/by-sa/2.0/>https://www.flickr.com/photos/xdxd_vs_xdxd/6829374609/in/photostream/

Exercise 2: Affirmations

Affirmations are positive statements that aim to rewire your brain and change your thoughts. Repeating them daily can help replace negative thoughts with positive ones and change how you view yourself and your past.

Write various affirmations on sticky notes and place them all over the house so you can repeat them throughout the day.

- I allow myself to heal.
- I am ready to make peace with my past.
- I am grateful for my strength.
- I am gently healing.

- I am willing to give and receive love.
- I am capable of unconditional love.
- I believe everything will be alright.
- I am making peace with myself and my past.
- I am happy and healthy.
- I let go of the past.
- I believe what's coming is good for me.
- I treat myself and others with kindness.
- I bless the past and embrace the present.
- I attract healthy relationships.
- I am grateful for myself.
- I always choose love.
- I manifest joy and healing.
- I deserve to be happy.
- I let go of grudges and choose forgiveness.
- I am a warrior.
- I am confident in my abilities.
- I am growing every day.
- I make self-care a priority.
- I am open to bettering myself.
- I radiate positivity.
- I am at peace with myself.
- I am open to receiving healing energy.
- Love and positivity flow through my body.
- I have compassion for myself and others.
- I reflect on my past with compassion.
- I am in charge of my life.
- I listen to my body's needs.

Write down a series of positive affirmations tailored to your insecurities or fears stemming from your disorganized attachment.

_____
_____
_____

Exercise 3: Healing Meditation

Instructions:

1. Find a quiet room in your home.
2. Sit in a comfortable position.
3. Think of a negative incident from your past or a negative emotion you are struggling with and want to overcome.
4. Close your eyes.
5. Take long, deep breaths through your nose and breathe out through your mouth for one or two minutes.
6. Visualize a large ball of white light radiating compassion, strength, healing power, and positive energy. (You can also visualize a cloud, a grandmotherly figure, or any image that makes you comfortable).
7. This figure envelops you in a blanket of security, acceptance, and love.
8. It is protecting you and you feel safe and empowered with its love.
9. Now, you are ready to face your difficult memory or emotion.
10. Face it, acknowledge it, and label it.
11. You aren't afraid of it. You feel safe being enveloped in the compassionate figure.
12. Its wisdom and kindness are flowing through you.

13. It starts speaking to comfort and reassure you, "Everything will be okay. You are strong, you are enough, and you are loved. You aren't alone. I am here with you, and we will get through this together."

14. (You can add more reassuring statements. Let the figure tell you anything you want to hear until you feel calm).

15. Thoughts inside your head are slowing down, tension in your body is melting away, and you feel calm and relaxed.

16. Negative emotions no longer have any power over you.

17. Whenever you face a challenging situation or a dark thought, visualize the compassionate figure wrapping its arms around you and making you feel safe.

Look at yourself in the mirror. What do you see? A person who has been through a traumatic experience, yet you are still standing. If you survive this trauma, you can also heal and grow.

You are stronger than you think and have the power to change your life and move on from the past. Believe in yourself and your abilities, celebrate each milestone, and acknowledge your wounds.

Don't allow your pain to define you. You aren't broken; you are healing. One day, you will recover and find your way back to yourself. Just be patient and keep going.

Section 5: Building Blocks of Trust: Creating a Secure Foundation

Trust sustains secure and thriving relationships. It is the foundation upon which emotional safety and connection are constructed. As you navigate relationships, trust is the invisible thread weaving through shared experiences, consistent actions, and the mutual respect you bring to the table. Its presence allows you to unveil your true self, expressing thoughts and feelings without fear of judgment or betrayal. These relationships become a sanctuary where you can be comfortable and authentically yourself.

Conversely, the absence of trust can cause cracks in a relationship's foundation. Suspicion and doubt may erode the bonds, leading to communication breakdowns and emotional distancing. Once disrupted, repairing trust demands a delicate touch, consistent effort, and a genuine commitment to rebuilding the bridge that reconnects you with people.

In your journey through relationships, see trust as a living force that breathes life into your connections. It guides you through the nuanced landscapes of human interaction, influencing your bonds' strength, depth, and resilience. It's not merely about understanding the importance of trust but actively engaging in the process of building and maintaining it. Your consistent efforts can create a space where you can authentically share and thrive.

22 Ways to Build More Trust in Your Relationships

Trust is something that is built and nurtured over time with communication and action.
Attribution 2.0 Generic, CC BY 2.0 DEED <https://creativecommons.org/licenses/by/2.0/>
https://www.flickr.com/photos/182229932@N07/48387126437

1. Open and Honest Communication

Establish a foundation of trust by practicing transparent and honest communication. Share your thoughts, feelings, and concerns openly, and encourage your partner to do the same to reduce misunderstandings. For example, openly express your feelings about a specific issue instead of hiding your feelings. Say you felt hurt when your partner canceled a plan without much notice. Politely express your concerns and advice to find a solution for next time.

2. Consistency in Actions

Trust is built over time through consistent behavior. Ensure your actions align with your words and commitments. Reliability and predictability create a sense of security, reinforcing the belief that you can be counted on.

3. Active Listening

Active listening shows you value and respect your partner's perspective. Make a conscious effort to understand their emotions, needs, and concerns. This not only strengthens communication but also shows that you genuinely care.

4. Setting and Respecting Boundaries

Establishing and adhering to boundaries helps is a sign of safety and mutual respect. Recognize and communicate your boundaries while being mindful of your partner's limits.

5. Vulnerability

Build trust by being vulnerable and allowing your partner to do the same. Sharing fears, insecurities, and aspirations creates a deep emotional connection. It signals that you trust them enough to reveal your authentic self.

6. Apologizing and Forgiving

Acknowledge mistakes and apologize when necessary. Equally important is the ability to forgive. Cultivate an environment where apologies are sincere and forgiveness is genuine.

7. Reliability

Follow through consistently on your commitments, no matter how small. Being reliable builds trust by demonstrating that you can be depended upon. It also reinforces the idea that your words carry weight and that you prioritize the relationship over other matters. For example, follow through when you promise to help with a task.

8. Shared Goals and Values

Aligning your goals and values with your partner's gives you a shared purpose. It ensures you are moving in the same direction, creating a deeper connection based on common aspirations. Discuss your long-term plans regularly. For example, if you were thinking about the future, you could check in with your partner to make sure the trajectory aligns with the goals you both have set.

9. Empathy

Understand and validate your partner's emotions. Try putting yourself in their shoes, acknowledging their feelings, and responding compassionately.

10. Consistent Support

Be a reliable source of support in both good times and bad. Consistency in being there for your partner strengthens the bond of trust by demonstrating your commitment to their well-being and success.

11. Share Positive Feedback

Regularly expressing appreciation is a powerful way to build trust. Acknowledge your partner's strengths, efforts, and contributions, creating a positive and supportive environment.

12. Be Transparent About Intentions

Transparency is key in fostering trust. Convey your intentions, motives, and decision-making processes to your partner, ensuring openness and clarity in your interactions.

13. Create Rituals of Connection

Establishing rituals or routines strengthens the bond between partners. Daily check-ins, weekly dates, or shared activities are an excellent way to build connection, stability, and predictability in the relationship.

14. Navigate Challenges Together

Facing challenges as a team is essential for building trust. Collaborate with your partner to find solutions and navigate difficulties. Teamwork builds resilience and strengthens the partnership.

15. Encourage Personal Growth

Supporting and encouraging each other's personal growth is another effective method to increase trust. Both partners should feel empowered to pursue individual goals, contributing to a sense of trust in each other's journeys.

16. Establish Clear Communication Norms

Clearly defining communication norms is crucial. This includes how conflicts are resolved, how information is shared, and the overall expectations around communication.

17. Be Mindful of Your Words and Actions

Mindful communication involves being intentional about your words and actions. Consider the potential impact on your partner's feelings and overall trust. Thoughtful communication shows your goal is to respect and understand your partner.

18. Seek Professional Guidance if Needed

If trust issues persist, seeking the help of a relationship counselor or therapist can lead you toward a path to build trust. These professionals are well-versed in situations like these and have the right tools to address and resolve trust-related challenges.

Seeking professional help allows you to tap into areas you may not be aware of that are holding you back.

19. Be Patient and Understanding

Building trust takes time and patience. Trust is a gradual process that evolves with both partners' consistent effort and positive actions.

20. Maintain Personal Integrity

When building trust, never compromise on your principles and values. Keep your actions consistent and reinforce trust by demonstrating authenticity and reliability. Likewise, equally respect the personal integrity of your partner by respecting their values.

21. Prioritize Quality Time

Spending quality time together is vital. Engaging in activities that promote meaningful conversations and deepen the emotional bond contributes to closeness and connection.

22. Express Vulnerability

Sharing vulnerabilities and insecurities nurtures openness and mutual trust. Expressing vulnerability allows both partners to feel safe being themselves.

23. Let Go

Avoid clinging to past mistakes, as holding grudges will only limit the development of trust. Instead, aim to work together. If you argue with your partner, use kind language that shows you want to resolve the conflict and move forward. Avoid statements that place blame on your partner; instead, discuss how to avoid these types of arguments in the future as a team.

Trust Inventory Exercise

The Trust Inventory exercise is a reflective activity designed to help you explore and understand your experiences with trust in past relationships. You can identify patterns, emotions, and underlying beliefs by digging deep into scenarios and experiences where trust was either upheld or broken.

Instructions:

Create a Timeline

Begin by constructing a timeline of your past relationships. List the names or use identifiers for each significant relationship, along with the approximate duration of each. This representation will aid in organizing your reflections.

_____
_____
_____
_____
_____
_____
_____
_____
_____

Identify Trust Instances

Recall and jot down specific instances where trust played a role in each relationship. These instances can be positive (trust upheld) or harmful (trust broken). Provide details about the circumstances, actions, and emotions experienced during these moments.

_____
_____
_____
_____
_____
_____

_____
_____
_____
_____

Categorize Trust Experiences

Group your instances into communication, reliability, honesty, vulnerability, and support. This categorization makes identifying similar patterns and themes related to trust within your relationships easier. For example, you might notice a pattern of trust being eroded when communication breaks down.

_____
_____
_____
_____
_____
_____
_____
_____
_____
_____

Reflect on Patterns

Analyze your trust instances and look for patterns or trends across different relationships. Are there recurring themes in how trust was either built or eroded? Reflect on the impact of these patterns on your overall trust in relationships and consider how they might have influenced the course of each connection.

_____
_____
_____
_____
_____
_____
_____
_____
_____
_____
_____

Explore Emotional Responses

Reflect on your emotional responses during these instances. How did you feel in each situation? Were there specific triggers or circumstances that influenced your emotional reactions?

_____
_____
_____
_____
_____
_____
_____
_____

Identify Beliefs about Trust

Consider your beliefs or assumptions about trust based on your past experiences. Do you find it easy to trust others, or do you approach new relationships with caution?

_____
_____
_____
_____
_____
_____
_____
_____

Set Positive Intentions

Based on your reflections, set positive intentions for building and maintaining trust in future relationships. Identify specific actions or behaviors you can incorporate to enhance trust in yourself and your interactions with others. This step is about proactively shaping a more positive and intentional approach to trust.

_____
_____
_____
_____
_____
_____
_____
_____

Create Trust-Building Strategies

Develop practical strategies for building trust in your current or future relationships. These strategies could include improving communication, setting clear expectations, or practicing vulnerability. Revamp these strategies to address the patterns and beliefs you've identified in your trust inventory.

_____
_____
_____
_____
_____
_____
_____
_____
_____

Monitor Progress

Periodically revisit your trust inventory as you navigate new relationships. Use it to monitor your progress, celebrate successes, and adjust as needed. Continuous self-reflection is key to building and maintaining healthy trust dynamics over time.

Trust-Building Commitments Activity

When done correctly, this practical exercise can enable you to develop and enhance trust in your current relationships. Committing to specific, actionable practices paves the way for cultivating a consistent pattern of trust-building actions, ultimately strengthening the relational foundation.

Instructions:

Self-Reflection

Begin by introspecting on your current relationships. Consider the dynamics, communication styles, and the level of trust you currently experience. Identify specific areas where trust could be improved or reinforced.

_____
_____
_____
_____
_____

Identify Trust-Building Actions

Make a list of actions or behaviors that are known to build trust. Examples include consistent communication, keeping small promises, active listening without judgment, sharing vulnerabilities, and demonstrating reliability.

Prioritize Actions

Evaluate and prioritize the identified trust-building actions based on their relevance to your relationships. Consider which actions are most aligned with your goals and have the potential for a significant positive impact.

Set Achievable Goals

Break down each trust-building action into smaller, achievable goals. For example, if consistent communication is a goal, set a specific target for how many times per week you will check in with your partner.

Create a Trust-Building Plan

Develop a detailed plan for implementing these actions. Specify when, where, and how you will carry out each commitment. A concrete plan gives you clarity and increases the likelihood of successfully turning intentions into tangible behaviors.

Accountability Measures

Establish accountability measures to track your progress. Accountability helps you stay focused on your goals. This could involve self-reflection, journaling, or sharing your commitments with a trusted friend or partner who can provide support and encouragement.

Monitor and Adjust

Regularly assess your progress in implementing trust-building actions. Be open to adjusting your commitments based on what is working well and what may need refinement. Be open and adjust to the evolving nature of relationships.

Celebrate Successes

Acknowledge and celebrate small and large successes. Recognize the positive impact your trust-building commitments have on your relationships.

14. Make it a point to celebrate milestones where you achieve a goal.

https://www.pexels.com/photo/person-pouring-wine-on-clear-drinking-glass-5775052/

Brainstorming on Challenges

Brainstorm any challenges or setbacks encountered in implementing your commitments. Consider them opportunities for learning and growth, and use these experiences to refine your approach moving forward.

Continual Growth

Recognize that trust-building is an ongoing process. As you witness positive changes in your relationships, explore additional trust-building actions and commitments to maintain growth and deepen trust.

Shared Experience Journal Exercise

Objective:

The Shared Experience Journal exercise is designed to deepen the connection and build trust by creating a shared narrative between partners. Journaling together encourages vulnerability, understanding, and a sense of shared history.

Instructions:

Get Two Journals

Acquire two separate journals or notebooks designated for this exercise. Although you can verbally go through your shared experiences, the physical act of writing can enhance the personal connection to the shared experience.

Establish Journaling Time

Decide on a specific time during the day or week when both partners can sit down to journal. This could be in the morning, before bedtime, or during a dedicated date night. The objective is to set a specific time and stick to the routine.

Choose a Writing Prompt

Select a writing prompt that encourages personal reflection and sharing. For example, "Reflect on a challenging moment in your life and how it shaped you" or "Describe a dream or aspiration you have for the future."

Write Independently

During the designated journaling time, both partners must independently write in their journals based on the chosen prompt. Be honest and clear when writing down the experience.

Exchange Journals

After completing the entries, exchange journals with your partner. Take turns reading each other's reflections and exploring your partner's thoughts, experiences, and perspectives.

Discuss and Share

Following the journal exchange, engage in a discussion about the entries. Share your thoughts and feelings about what you wrote and what you learned from your partner's reflections. Be open to discussing emotions and experiences.

Identify Common Themes

Look for common themes, shared values, or similar experiences from journal entries. Identifying these common themes builds a sense of connection, understanding, and trust through shared narratives.

Set New Writing Prompts

Rotate the responsibility of choosing writing prompts. As you become comfortable sharing your experiences with your partner, be creative and select prompts that highlight the different aspects of personal and shared experiences.

Create a Symbolic Gesture

Introduce a symbolic gesture to accompany the shared experience journaling process. This could be a specific object placed near the journals or a particular ritual to mark the beginning and end of each session.

Reflect on Trust Building

Periodically, reflect on how the shared experience journal exercise has influenced trust in your relationship. Discuss any communication, understanding, or emotional connection changes emerging from this shared narrative-building process.

Understanding Trust Cues

Understanding trust cues is essential for your relationship. Trust cues are the subtle signals and indicators that make or break the trust between you and your partner. These cues encompass various aspects of communication, behavior, and interactions that influence how trust is perceived and maintained.

In your relationship, trust cues may include non-verbal communication, such as sharing concerns through body language, facial expressions, and tone of voice. Pay attention to these cues, which can convey important information about your partner's intentions, emotions, and trustworthiness.

Furthermore, watch for trust cues linked to verbal communication and actions. Notice how your partner follows through on commitments, keeps promises, and communicates openly and honestly with you. Consistency in behavior, transparency, and reliability are more positive trust cues that establish a secure relationship foundation.

On the other hand, be mindful of trust-diminishing cues, such as inconsistencies in behavior, evasiveness, or dishonesty. These cues only damage trust and create doubt or uncertainty in your relationship. Recognizing and addressing trust-diminishing cues helps maintain a healthy level of trust between you and your partner.

Being attuned to trust cues makes you more aware of the trust dynamics within your relationship. The verbal and non-verbal cues you pay attention to give you valuable insights into the level of trust between you and your partner. Effective communication and mutual understanding of these trust cues can easily build a secure and trusting foundation in your relationship.

Forgiveness and Rebuilding

Relationships go through difficult times where you or your partner can make a wrong move, compromising the trust. Forgiveness and rebuilding trust are crucial when trust has been compromised in your relationship. Forgiveness is your deliberate and conscious decision to release feelings of resentment or anger toward someone who has caused harm.

When trust is broken, the process of rebuilding relies on open communication, transparency, and a commitment to change. Both you and your partner need to engage in honest discussions about the breach of trust, its impact, and the necessary steps for moving forward. Rebuilding trust requires your willingness to acknowledge mistakes, take responsibility, and demonstrate consistent and positive changes in behavior.

Remember that forgiveness does not mean forgetting or excusing the behavior that led to the breach of trust. Instead, it involves letting go of negative emotions and working towards rebuilding the relationship. Successful rebuilding of trust may require you to set clear boundaries, establish expectations for future behavior, and create an environment where you and your partner feel safe and understood.

Crisis and Trust Resilience

Significant challenges or events can potentially threaten the stability and trust between you and your partner. Crisis situations may include issues like infidelity, major life changes, financial difficulties, or serious health concerns, to name a few.

Trust resilience is your relationship's ability to withstand and recover from such crises. It requires you, with your partner, to navigate challenges, adapt to new circumstances, and emerge from the crisis with a strengthened sense of trust. Trust resilience is not about avoiding challenges but confronting them together and using the experience to deepen your connection.

During a crisis, effective communication becomes even more critical. You and your partner must openly discuss your feelings, concerns, and expectations, providing support and understanding to each other. Trust resilience requires your shared commitment to working through the difficulties, learning from the experience, and reinforcing the foundation of trust in your relationship.

Building trust resilience involves acknowledging vulnerabilities, seeking external support if needed (such as counseling or therapy), and finding constructive ways to cope with the emotional impact of the crisis. Successfully navigating a crisis can lead to a deeper level of trust as you witness each other's commitment and resilience in the face of adversity.

Still, it might be difficult for some people to create a secure foundation of trust. In situations like these, involving a professional therapist is necessary as they can enable you to steer the trajectory of your relationships toward building trust, compassion, and understanding while keeping your distinct habits, behaviors, and needs in mind.

Section 6: Communication: Establishing Understanding

Effective communication is the foundation for developing understanding and connection with others. This chapter highlights the impact of honing communication skills, recognizing their transformative power, and emphasizing their paramount importance, especially for people with disorganized attachment.

The best way to gain a deeper understanding to avoid disorganized attachment is to communicate effectively.

https://www.pexels.com/photo/cheerful-multiracial-couple-looking-at-each-other-3776877/

When used correctly, communication is a magical concoction capable of dissolving misunderstandings, promoting empathy, and nurturing authentic connections. Communication becomes even more crucial for people facing challenges forming secure emotional bonds. It can mend fractured connections and build bridges to emotional security.

Effective communication is not limited to the exchange of words. It is a skill involving active listening, empathetic understanding, and the ability to express oneself. Its effective communication builds solid connections in relationships and makes it easier to navigate the labyrinth of emotions and experiences.

Besides creating deeper bonds and an emotionally sound environment, communication can lead to healing. As you already know, attachment patterns formed in early relationships can shape your ability to relate to others later in life. When it comes to disorganized attachment, the inconsistent caregiving or traumatic experiences you experienced can create barriers to forming secure connections. Surprisingly, using the transformative power of effective communication, it's possible to rewrite the narrative of these relationships and keep you on a consistent path toward mental and emotional stability.

This chapter will explore practical strategies for enhancing communication skills tailored to anyone with disorganized attachment. From navigating challenging conversations to building a foundation of trust, each section aims to equip you with the right information to navigate the delicate nuances of human connection. As you continue this journey, remember that communication is your tool for transformation, a vessel that carries you from isolation to intimacy and from misunderstanding to profound connection.

Active Listening Role-Play

Communication goes both ways, and one of the foundational stones for building strong connections is active listening. Although you are expressing yourself to others, you must also lend an ear, especially in relationships.

This role-playing exercise significantly improves your active listening skills. Before starting the exercise, ensure you are comfortable and safe.

Instructions:

Pair Up

Find a partner for the activity. If you're in a group, form pairs.

Choose a Speaker

Decide who will be the speaker and who will be the listener for the first round.

Select a Topic

The speaker selects a topic to discuss for a few minutes. It could be something personal, a hobby, a recent experience, or anything they feel comfortable sharing.

Set a Timer

Use a timer to allocate a specific time frame (3-5 minutes) for the speaker to talk. The activity must be structured, allowing the participants equal opportunities to share and discuss the topic.

Switch Roles

After the allotted time, switch roles. The listener becomes the speaker, and the speaker becomes the listener. This allows each participant to experience both sides of the conversation.

Active Listening

When you are listening, your primary focus should be on the speaker. Avoid interrupting, offering advice, or sharing your own experiences during their turn. Instead, use non-verbal cues like nodding, making eye contact, and leaning slightly forward to show engagement.

Summarize and Validate

After the speaker has shared, the listener summarizes what they heard. This step is not about testing anyone's memory but understanding and validating the speaker's feelings and experiences. Ask questions for clarification and try to capture the essence of what was shared. The speaker can also add more to the questions asked for further clarification.

Reflect

The participants must now share their experiences. Discuss how it felt to be the speaker and the listener. Note down any challenges or insights you gained about your communication styles.

By the end of this activity, you will have learned more about your communication style, how you connect to others, and the areas of communication that might need improvement. This activity also cultivates deep listening skills, further promoting a genuine understanding of communication styles.

Communication Style Self-Assessment

Although you need to choose what to say when trying to communicate effectively, it is equally important to know how to say it. Understanding your dominant communication style improves your interactions with others. This self-assessment asks you a series of questions to help identify whether your communication style is assertive, passive, aggressive, or passive-aggressive.

Instructions:

Choose the response that most accurately reflects your typical behavior for each question. Don't hold back; be honest with yourself to understand your communication tendencies clearly. Add up your scores at the end to identify your dominant style.

When expressing your needs or opinions:

- I am direct and clear about what I want.
- I often hold back to avoid conflict.
- I tend to dominate the conversation and may not listen to others.
- I express myself indirectly, leaving my true feelings unclear.

How do you handle criticism or feedback?

- I appreciate constructive feedback and use it to improve.
- I take it personally and may become defensive.
- I respond with aggression or anger.
- I might agree outwardly but harbor resentment.

In a conflict situation, your initial reaction is to:

- Address the issue openly and seek a resolution.
- Avoid confrontation and hope the problem resolves on its own.
- Confront the other person forcefully.
- Express dissatisfaction indirectly or through sarcasm.

When making decisions in a group:

- I actively participate and voice my opinions.

- I go along with the majority to avoid conflict.
- I often impose my ideas on others.
- I may agree outwardly but resist internally.

Your body language tends to be:
- Open, confident, and engaged.
- Reserved, avoiding eye contact.
- Assertive, possibly with intense gestures.
- Passive, with subtle signs of frustration.

Scoring:
- For every 'I am direct...' response, assign 4 points.
- For every 'I often hold back...' response, assign 3 points.
- For every 'I tend to dominate...' response, assign 2 points.
- For every 'I express myself indirectly...' response, assign 1 point.

Interpretation:
- 16-20 points: Assertive Communicator
- 11-15 points: Passive Communicator
- 6-10 points: Aggressive Communicator
- 5 or below: Passive-Aggressive Communicator

After you have completed the scoring, take a moment to consider how your dominant communication style impacts your relationships and interactions. This can help you better tweak your communication style.

The Empathy Mirror

Empathy is vital to effective communication because it develops understanding and connection. In this reflective activity, you'll step into the shoes of others and learn to empathize and communicate more compassionately.

Instructions:

Select a Partner

Team up with a partner for this activity. It works best to find someone you are comfortable with and trust.

Define Roles

Decide who will be the speaker and who will be the listener first. You'll switch roles later.

Choose a Personal Experience

The speaker selects a personal experience or emotion they would like to share. It could be a joyful moment, a challenging experience, or an emotion they often grapple with.

Express Yourself

The speaker takes a few minutes to express their chosen experience or emotion. Be genuine and open about your thoughts and feelings. Share as much or as little as you feel comfortable.

Listener's Role

This step is the most crucial in this activity. If you are the listener, your task will be to mirror what you understand about the speaker's experience. Focus on the speaker's emotions and thoughts and respond accordingly.

The listener has to actively listen to understand the tone and message given through the conversation.

Reflective responses can be:

- "It sounds like..."
- "I sense that..."
- "You feel..."

• "It must be challenging/exciting/frustrating for you..."

Switch Roles

After the first round, switch roles. The speaker becomes the listener, and vice versa.

Open Discussion

Take some time to discuss the experience. How did it feel to express yourself? How did it feel to have your experience mirrored back to you? What insights did you gain about the power of empathetic communication?

Consider how this activity influenced your understanding of empathetic communication. Did you feel more connected to your partner? How might incorporating reflective listening into daily interactions enhance your communication skills and deepen your relationships?

With continuous practice of empathetic communication, you can strengthen your ability to understand and connect with others on a deeper level.

Mirrored Drawing

This creative and interactive activity encourages non-verbal communication and cooperation. It's an engaging way to explore the subtleties of understanding and working together.

Instructions:

Pick a family member, friend, partner, or peer for this drawing activity.

Materials Needed

Gather drawing materials like paper, pencils, markers, or any artistic tools you prefer. Ensure each person has a separate set of materials.

Set the Scene

Choose a quiet space where you can both comfortably sit facing each other. The idea is to maintain eye contact and view each other's drawings.

Mirror Drawing

Decide who will be the drawer and who will be the mirror. The drawer will create a simple drawing, and the mirror will replicate it simultaneously without seeing the original.

Start Drawing

The drawer begins by creating a basic drawing, keeping it simple yet distinct. It could be an object, a shape, or even an abstract design. Ensure it's not too intricate to allow for easy replication.

Mirror and Replicate

Without showing the drawing to the mirror, the drawer describes it verbally. The mirror listens carefully and replicates the description on their own paper.

Switch Roles

After the first round, switch roles. The previous mirror becomes the drawer, and vice versa. Repeat the process with a new drawing.

Review and Discuss

Once both drawings are complete, compare the original and mirrored versions. Discuss the challenges, successes, and insights gained during the activity.

Non-Verbal Cues

Explore the non-verbal cues you both picked up during the activity. Did eye contact, facial expressions, or gestures enhance or hinder communication?

Discuss Takeaways

Engage in a conversation about the experience. What did you learn about your communication styles? How did non-verbal cues impact the overall understanding? What strategies could improve collaborative efforts?

Reflect

Reflect on how the Mirrored Drawing activity highlighted non-verbal communication and collaboration nuances. Consider how these insights can enhance your verbal and non-verbal communication in various aspects of your relationship.

The Perspective Swap

Understanding different perspectives is another cornerstone of effective communication. This activity focuses on improving empathy and broadening your understanding of diverse viewpoints.

Instructions:

Choose a Partner

Pair up with a partner. It can be a friend, family member, or colleague.

Identify a Situation

Each participant thinks of a recent situation or experience where they had a differing opinion or perspective from the other. It could be related to work, personal life, or a shared experience.

Express Your Perspective

The first participant shares their perspective on the chosen situation. If you are going first, describe your thoughts, emotions, and reasons behind your viewpoint.

Active Listening

The other participant actively listens without interrupting. When you become the listener, take note of the key points, emotions, and any details that stand out. Do remember to switch roles accordingly.

Reflective Questions

Engage in a discussion using reflective questions. Examples include:

- How did it feel to express your perspective?
- What surprised you about the other person's viewpoint?
- Did you discover any common ground or shared feelings?

Find Common Ground

Explore areas of agreement or shared emotions. Identify common ground that can be a foundation for understanding and future communication.

Discuss Communication Strategies

Share communication strategies that could have improved the understanding of each other's perspectives in the given situation.

Reflect

Take some time to reflect on the activity. How did it feel to express and listen to different perspectives? What did you learn about effective communication and understanding in this process?

This activity strengthens your ability to see situations from different angles and encourages open dialogue.

Power of Improved Communication

Think of improved communication as your personal key to unlocking the doors of connection, understanding, and authentic relationships.

Understanding the Significance

For you, improved communication isn't just about words; it's about creating a bridge that brings people closer. When you communicate effectively, you express thoughts and emotions and invite others into the authentic sanctuary of who you are.

Fostering Deeper Connections

Consider your relationships as gardens that flourish with care and attention. Your improved communication acts as sunlight, nurturing seeds of understanding and trust. By expressing yourself authentically and listening empathetically, your connections will thrive through shared experiences and mutual respect.

Navigating the Complexity

Your relationships are intricate, with nuances that require delicate handling. Improved communication equips you with the tools to navigate the labyrinth of emotions, resolve conflicts constructively, and strengthen the bonds forming the foundation of your connections. It's a skill set that transforms misunderstandings into opportunities for growth and challenges into stepping stones toward deeper intimacy.

The Timeless Opportunity

As you reflect on this journey of enhancing your communication skills, remember it's never too late to embark on this path. Whether you're at the dawn of self-discovery or amidst the seasoned chapters of your life, the opportunity to build and refine your communication skills is ever-present.

The Wisdom of Beginning

Think of your communication skills as a garden you can cultivate at any stage of life. Just as a flower doesn't blossom overnight, the journey to effective communication is a gradual process that unfolds with patience, dedication, and self-reflection. Embrace the wisdom that each conversation, interaction, and exchange is a canvas on which you can paint the strokes of improvement. Furthermore, be transparent and authentic in your conversations, especially with family members, close friends, and loved ones. Clear communication lays the foundation for setting clear boundaries and developing mutual understanding.

Embracing Growth

By investing in your communication skills, you embrace growth, not just in your relationships but in your understanding of yourself. Celebrate the small victories, learn from the challenges, and let the improvement process be a testament to your commitment to connections that withstand the test of time.

The Tapestry of Tomorrow

As you refine your communication skills, your relationships evolve into vibrant masterpieces. Envision conversations that resonate with authenticity, understanding that transcends words, and resilient connections in the face of life's fluctuations.

Improving your communication skills is an investment in the quality of your relationships, and it's an investment with timeless returns. This is your evergreen opportunity to create connections that stand the sands of time and flourish with each passing season. So, embrace this journey, for the path to enriched relationships begins with the simple yet profound act of communicating with intention and heart.

Tips to Improve Communication

Active Listening:

Grant your full attention to the speaker, refrain from interruptions, and focus on comprehending their message before responding.

Empathy:

Work on a deeper connection by stepping into the shoes of others, earnestly seeking to understand their unique perspective, empathizing with their emotions, and acknowledging their needs.

Setting Boundaries:

Although you won't be setting boundaries with peers at your workplace or people you don't meet often, setting boundaries for improved communication is necessary in close relationships. Be open about your values, personal needs, and behaviors that make you feel uncomfortable. Setting boundaries enhances your relationships and makes people able to trust you.

Clarify and Confirm:

Inquire for clarification when someone says something that appears ambiguous. Confirm your comprehension of the message, eradicating any potential misunderstandings.

Avoid Assumptions:

Avoid presumptions about others' thoughts or feelings, opting instead for open-ended questions to explore their inner world and develop a deeper mutual understanding.

Be Mindful of Non-Verbal Cues:

Grasp the nuances of body language and facial expressions. Interpreting these subtle cues will help you understand someone's emotions and reactions.

Respect Differences:

Acknowledge and honor diverse communication styles and cognitive processes. Embrace a flexible approach that respects individual differences in expression and interpretation.

Stay Calm During Conflicts:

Strive for composure in the crucible of conflict. Resist the temptation to heighten tensions with raised voices or defensiveness. Take a temporary step back before reengaging with a clear mind if necessary.

Express Yourself Clearly:

Articulate your thoughts with precision and brevity, avoiding vague language. Give specific examples when expressing yourself to ensure others understand your perspective.

Regular Check-Ins:

Establish a routine of periodic check-ins where you can address concerns proactively, mitigating potential escalation. Don't conduct these check-ins when you're stressed or emotionally reactive. Address your concerns when you're calm.

Use Positive Reinforcement:

Express acknowledgment and appreciation for effective exchanges. Positive reinforcement encourages sustained efforts and contributes to a constructive communication atmosphere.

Honest Conversations:

Always be transparent about your feelings, thoughts, and needs. Be honest, authentic, and sincere when communicating without hiding relevant or important information. Furthermore, avoid lying, omitting crucial details, or deceiving others, as these only erode trust in relationships.

Seek Feedback:

Actively encourage others to share constructive feedback regarding your communication style. Leverage this valuable information to pinpoint areas for improvement and adapt your approach accordingly.

Cultural Sensitivity:

Be attuned to diverse communication styles. Embrace and adapt to varied ways of expressing ideas and emotions, boosting cross-cultural understanding.

Set Clear Expectations:

Clarify your expectations to mitigate potential misunderstandings. Encourage others to do the same so you're on the same page.

Be Patient:

Building understanding and effective communication is a gradual process. Be patient with yourself and others as you navigate the intricacies of relationship dynamics.

Besides working on understanding your communication patterns and improving your communication style, never push yourself to the edge if you are struggling. Past experiences, interactions, and relationships can affect how you communicate and perceive what others say. These experiences can also create a barrier that further deteriorates your communication. If you are still having problems with establishing communication, visiting a therapist or a certified health professional can assist you in exploring the reasons for your communication issues and addressing the distress or difficulty that comes with it.

Section 7: Self-Compassion and Inner-Healing

Unhealthy attachment patterns lead to giving yourself a hard time about doing something you regret. You may regret several actions from your relationships cultivated through maladaptive attachment. However, there is an alternative to beating yourself up for your inability to form healthier relationships. It's called being kind to yourself, better known as self-compassion.

Self-compassion allows for inner healing to take place.
https://www.pexels.com/photo/a-woman-in-beige-tank-top-sitting-on-yoga-mat-6246654/

Imagine living without that tough inner critic telling you what you're doing wrong. So what if you haven't crossed the milestones many others your age did? There are plenty of others in the same shoes you are. Maybe you haven't learned to resolve conflicts yet. You're getting there. Maybe you haven't grown to be the best version of yourself yet. What matters is that you're working on it. Being kind to yourself might sound cliche, but it's anything but. It's a powerful tool for healing.

You have a decision to make: Will you ignore the taunts of your inner critic or use self-compassion to silence its voice? If you opt for the latter, this chapter will give you a head start on a nurturing journey toward self-acceptance and healing from within.

What Is Self-Compassion?

Two powerful sisters rule over every person's life. They're called Compassion and Condemnation. Condemnation is loud and flashy, and she wants her opinions to be heard. For the same reason, she is very good at getting what she wants because most people give her control over themselves. Compassion, on the other hand, is unassuming and easily overpowered by her sister. People neglect her because she is so quiet they don't know if they can trust her. Unlike her sister, who points out flaws in everyone, Compassion helps people forgive themselves for their mistakes and imperfections. One day, Compassion asked Condemnation why she judges others unrelentingly. Condemnation became very sad and said she does this because it is all she can do. Her fault is that she doesn't know better. Compassion, being true to herself, said that it's okay to have faults and that Condemnation can learn to do many other things if she puts her mind to it.

Self-compassion is acting toward yourself as you would toward a sibling or friend who feels bad about their faults. It means showing support, acceptance, and understanding for yourself, just as you would to someone you love when they are going through a tough time. It also means you can accept that you won't lose motivation to try harder if you stop being critical of yourself. Quite the contrary, self-compassion is known to boost motivation, while self-criticism will make you anxious, which is a true motivation killer.

Have you noticed that instead of helping you work through your issues, your inner critic makes you procrastinate on getting started? This isn't a coincidence. Self-criticism triggers the stress posture in the body and mind, telling you that you're in danger and must preserve your strength by doing nothing. Compassionate inner talk does the opposite. It lowers cortisol and other stress levels, allowing you to focus on self-regulation in challenging situations.

Tip: You can learn to be kind to yourself by developing a more supportive dialogue to help you understand that your imperfections and failures don't define you. Cultivating this positive mindset takes practice in non-stressing situations, so you can apply it successfully when you don't perform well under stress.

The Importance of Self-Compassion in Healing

Those with attachment issues find it particularly challenging to show all that kindness, empathy, and love they shower on their loved ones *to themselves.* Instead, they become their biggest critics and end up punishing themselves. This is why self-compassion is so crucial in healing from unhealthy attachments.

"When we give ourselves compassion, we are opening our hearts in a way that can transform our lives." – **Kristin Neff**

Beyond helping you heal from past trauma, self-compassion can help lower your stress, enabling you to manage stressful situations better. By alleviating symptoms of anxiety and depression, the practice of being kind to yourself can become essential for your physical and mental health and well-being.

According to psychology professor Kristin Neff, self-compassion can be measured through the person's ability to:

- Understand that mistakes are a natural part of everyone's life and fully believe that everyone else encounters tough situations in which they make mistakes.
- Show understanding, tolerance, and patience toward their imperfections and errors, especially if these are shown in the face of adversity.
- Be aware of their emotions and remain objective about them when encountering a stressful situation.
- Maintain a sense of connectedness to those around them, even if they feel that they don't deserve to have relationships with

anyone.

- Avoid being harsh, disapproving, and judgmental of their inadequacies and shortcomings.
- Acknowledging and promptly releasing negative thoughts and emotions instead of just putting them in the back of their mind.

The six abilities affect people's lives and mental health in different ways. One reason this differentiation occurs lies in the early attachment patterns.

You may be wondering how attachments affect your ability to cultivate self-compassion. What you learn in attachment relationships in early childhood will lay the foundation for how you interact with the world later on. It will also cause you to form a strong perception of yourself and your attitude toward yourself.

In other words, you as an adult will likely treat yourself the same way your parents or caregivers treated you during early childhood. If they were compassionate, loving, and comforting when you felt overwhelmed or distressed, you'd learn to be the same way to yourself. You would likely do the same if you were treated without much affection and told to "get over it" whenever you felt upset.

Attachment is linked to how people navigate emotions, which is also learned by example in childhood. If the adults in your life showed positive examples of managing one's emotions, you've learned to cope with them. Suppose the only example you saw was avoiding and repressing emotions and resorting to unhealthy coping mechanisms. In that case, this is what you'll emulate later.

Self-compassion has much to do with the example you've grown up with. How you respond to negative thoughts and emotions is rooted in the ability to tolerate, understand, and manage these.

Conversely, the link between self-compassion and attachment is a two-way street. Parents who are empathetic and accepting toward a child's feelings and beliefs foster a secure connection between themselves and the child. You'll have poor emotional regulation skills if you've grown up without experiencing the sense of warmth, openness, and reassurance of a healthy bond. Consequently, you'll have a lower capacity to cultivate self-compassion in adult relationships.

A Lesson from a Child

A dad who acts as his young son's sports coach explains how his own little boy taught him a lesson of self-compassion. As he says, he was preparing to make a move, which he unfortunately missed. He says he became very angry at himself because it was something he wanted to show his child how to do. Missing it made him feel inadequate, which he voiced out loud. He says that when his son heard him saying to himself that he couldn't believe he had made that mistake, his son immediately said to stop saying that. The little boy said that everyone makes mistakes and that he was sure his dad would do better next time. The dad was incredibly proud of his son for saying this because he had taught him this since they began training. At the same time, he was incredibly humbled that he also needed to be reminded of this.

And it's not just how adults treat children that will affect how they treat themselves in adulthood. How adults treat themselves will also be seen as an example to emulate.

"If you can love, love yourself first." **Charles Bukowski**

How you establish your relationship with yourself determines how you connect with others. Being kind to yourself will give you a glimpse of how your personal relationships will look like.

By acknowledging that you'll make mistakes and sometimes act in a way you'll regret later, you'll see yourself from a different perspective, which can help build meaningful connections. You can be honest about how you relate to others because you know how you relate to yourself. By caring for yourself through self-compassion practices, you'll learn how to care for others lovingly and appropriately instead of resorting to unhealthy attachment patterns. You'll have a more constant and steady feeling of self-worth, translating into how you relate to aspects like social approval, pressure, and norms.

If you have attachment issues, this may foreshadow a bleak future. After all, if being compassionate to yourself is a skill to understand, tolerate, and manage negative emotions effectively, and all these become difficult for you, how can there be a way out?

The answer to this question can be found in the link between attachment and self-compassion. The lack of the latter relates to you having a hard time being kind to yourself, being judgmental or cold to yourself, and your lack of self-awareness. You may even have very few warm thoughts of yourself, which can lead to anxiety, depression, and an overall lower quality of life.

The key to cultivating self-compassion beyond attachment is to overturn the negative aspects. Instead of coldness, there should be warmness. Instead of self-criticism should be self-acceptance and motivation. By cultivating a positive self-image, you can overcome unhealthy attachments and complete the transformative journey of inner healing.

"The most terrifying thing is to accept oneself completely." **Carl Jung**

A positive self-image is a cornerstone of self-compassion because it allows you to see yourself in a warmer light and assess the true magnitude of your mistakes and inadequacies instead of overestimating them. This doesn't mean minimizing your shortcomings or failures.

While immensely powerful, cultivating a positive self-image is only one of the steps you can take to heal. Working on how you see yourself will not automatically quit your inner critic. It will still be there, but there are other avenues you can take to minimize their effect on you. In the continuation of this chapter, you'll find exercises that will help you complete your healing journey and become the most self-compassionate version of yourself you've ever been.

Writing to Your Younger Self

Writing is a powerful self-expression tool that can help you reflect on points you may feel stuck in during your healing journey. It can also open up a dialogue where you can address your younger self, who needed the compassion it never had, with understanding, love, and forgiveness.

Writing a letter to your younger self is incredibly therapeutic.
https://www.pexels.com/photo/person-holding-pen-261599/

This powerful exercise helps you acknowledge past pains and offer self-compassion, fostering a sense of healing and closure. Remember that the process will trigger powerful emotions, so if you need to stop at any time, feel free to do that. You can always pick up and continue where you left off.

One of the easiest ways to address this aspect of yourself is through a letter titled:

A Letter to My Younger Self

Start by addressing your younger self in a kind and compassionate way. Think about your experience when you were younger. What was it that you would've wanted to hear back then?

Write a few lines reflecting on your experiences from this age. How have they shaped who you are now?

If any emotions resurface related to this experience, name and acknowledge them. Your younger self should know you can embrace anything, be it pain, heartache, fear, regret, or anything else.

Share the lessons you've learned from your later experiences and offer advice to your younger self. Encourage them to be more honest and vulnerable, and don't be afraid to do the same.

Acknowledge that there are things you wish you would've known when you were their age, but tell them you can't change anything. Whether you were driven by misguided values, unrealistic social expectations, or not-so-ideal attachment models, you shouldn't let your past decisions define you.

Remind your younger self that they are loved because they are worthy of it. They are strong and resilient, even if they don't believe they are. Tell them all the qualities you admire about them and how proud you are of them.

You can add anything else you want in your letter and close it with a heartfelt message of compassion.

Daily Gratitude and Self-Compassion Journaling

A daily practice of writing down three things you're grateful for about yourself each day and a statement of self-compassion is a wonderful way to foster both. It's a routine that aims to shift focus towards positive self-recognition and nurture a kinder self-dialogue.

Journaling is one of the most effective ways to convey one's emotions, especially for those who find talking about their feelings too intimidating. For the best effects, making your entries during the evening is recommended. You can reflect on the day's events and find what you feel grateful for and why you deserve to be kind to yourself. This can be anything you often judge yourself for or something that causes you pain you can't get over.

Further prompts on formulating your gratitude and self-compassion entries include writing mindfully, showing kindness to yourself, and relying on common humanity.

It's not always easy to find something to be grateful for when everything seems to go wrong. In challenging circumstances, the last thing you can conjure into your mind will be a meaningful statement of compassion. This is where mindfulness comes in. It will help you bring awareness to the painful emotions without allowing them to distract you from the task at hand. Acknowledge how you feel, and embrace these feelings without judgment. For example, if you were rude to someone that day, accept that you were frustrated and that this happens to everyone. If you feel that you would have reacted differently, your gratitude entry could be about being happy that you can now see where you need to make changes.

Self-kindness entails comforting yourself. Ensure your tone is gentle and reassuring, especially when writing the self-compassion statement. Tell yourself that whatever mistake you make, it will all be okay. Whatever experiences you had that made you feel bad, they will be better next time.

Acknowledge that being human means you'll have flaws because everyone does. They also have bad experiences. Remember, negative experiences are wonderful learning opportunities, just like mistakes are. So, be grateful to have them because each will bring you a step closer to healing and growth.

A regular gratitude and self-compassion journal will help you organize your thoughts and feelings. Moreover, the more positive and motivating you are, the more these become engraved in your subconscious, where they can translate into your day-to-day life.

Embrace the Healing Power of Self-Kindness

"Loving yourself isn't vanity. It's sanity." **Katrina Mayer**

A lack of self-compassion can harm your health and well-being in many ways. Beyond creating emotional distress and the accompanying physical distress, it can make maintaining healthy relationships nearly impossible. This can bleed into your personal and private life, hindering your growth and development. It can aggravate your attachment issues and make healing from unhealthy patterns all the more difficult.

Everyone experiences challenges in life and relationships. Losing a job, ending a romantic relationship, or losing touch with a dear friend or family member can all be devastating. However, with self-compassion, you can cultivate positive emotions amid these adversities and form a more realistic picture of your circumstances.

Self-compassion has a therapeutic effect combined with other approaches and as a standalone practice. It can immensely heal relationships you have with yourself and others. At the same time, by developing healthier attachment styles, you can boost your self-esteem, hone your strengths, and ultimately, be more kind to yourself.

It's normal to lack confidence in one's abilities from time to time, but when you do it all the time, it becomes problematic. By practicing self-kindness, you can prevent this from becoming a norm.

Forming an inner dialogue can be a foreign concept to many. However, you may not realize that you already have this conversation every time you listen to your inner critic. When you heed its "advice," it looks more like a monologue, in which you are addressing yourself in a way you would probably never address a friend. It's up to you to turn this into a dialogue where you can actively respond and refute the negative narratives your inner critic feeds you. By practicing self-compassion, you can become your best friend instead of being your worst enemy.

With regular practice, self-compassion can become your north star. Instead of blaming yourself when you make a mistake, notice an imperfection, or become affected by a negative experience, your first reaction will be to be kind to yourself. This is one of the biggest transformations self-kindness will bring into your life.

Make the effort to convert self-compassion into a daily self-care ritual. When you feel unsure, stressed, upset, or any other negative emotions throughout the day, reach for a few kind words you can say to yourself.

Or, it can be as simple as doing something you enjoy just because you deserve it (even if you don't feel like you did). It will be much easier to find a solution to whatever triggered the feelings when they aren't clouding your mind. You'll be calmer, and instead of your weaknesses, you'll be able to hone in on your strengths.

Self-compassion is a valuable skill that will positively impact your ability to find happiness. Wouldn't you agree that it's a practice worth pursuing on your healing journey for all these reasons?

Section 8: Developing Healthy Relationships

You have probably heard of the TV show Friends. It's about six flawed individuals from different backgrounds who have created an unbreakable bond. They are always there for each other, providing advice, love, and support. They can always count on the other five if one is in need. Most people who watch this show aspire to have this kind of friendship.

The key to developing healthy relationships is to learn how to create unbreakable bonds.
https://www.pexels.com/photo/men-s-white-button-up-dress-shirt-708440/

Everyone needs people they can count on who make them feel less alone. Your trauma has probably impacted your ability to trust anyone. Part of your healing is learning to establish healthy and strong relationships based on mutual respect and trust.

This section provides strategies, tips, and activities for understanding and developing healthy relationship dynamics.

What Makes a Healthy Relationship?

Healthy relationships are built on open communication, trust, honesty, and respect. They involve compromise and effort from you and your partner, friend, or family member. You respect each other's independence, space, feelings, and wishes.

You handle conflicts with love and respect. You feel safe around them because you know they won't push you to do things that make you uncomfortable. You can express yourself without fear of judgment, and you encourage each other to follow your passions and dreams.

Healthy relationships bring joy and peace, unlike toxic individuals, who drain your energy and make you dread being around them.

Positivity

You should feel uplifted around the people in your life. They should be affectionate towards you and make you feel good. Whether it's your partner, family, friends, or co-workers, they should treat you kindly and meet you with a smile unless they are having a bad day.

Honesty

Honesty involves always saying the truth and compassionately expressing yourself without hurting the other person's feelings. It's being direct instead of saying half-truths or omitting certain details.

In healthy relationships, you should always be your authentic self and never hide any parts of yourself.

Balance

Balanced relationships involve putting in equal effort. In romantic relationships, you and your partner put in the work and time to make your relationship work. You both call and text each other, make plans to spend time together, and equally invest in the relationship.

In friendships, you and your friends make time for each other and are always there for one another. In professional relationships, balance or equality doesn't usually exist in a hierarchical environment. However, you should find acknowledgment and respect at work.

Respect

Mutual respect is key in any relationship. Respect each other's boundaries, time, opinions, decisions, strengths, and contributions. Appreciate them for their unique qualities and acknowledge their value and significance in your life. They should also treat you with the same respect and make you feel special.

Support

Life isn't always easy. It will help to have someone by your side to support you and have your back. They should celebrate your victories, push you to pursue your goals, celebrate your milestones, and believe in you. You should treat your loved ones the same way, always be there for them when they need you, and be their biggest cheerleader.

Trust

You can't build a healthy relationship without trust. You should take your time to know each other and cultivate an open relationship based on honesty and mutual trust.

Signs of Unhealthy Relationships

- Controlling behavior
- Yelling
- Unequal power (for instance, one person can have control over the other's finances or decisions)
- Poor communication
- Sacrificing your needs to make the other person happy
- Having no control over your privacy
- Turning tables during conflicts
- Feeling pressured to spend all your time with them
- Feeling unaccepted and pressured to change
- Criticism over everything you do and say and the way you dress
- Trying to keep you away from your family or friends to make it easier to control you
- Acting condescending towards your job and passions
- Walking on eggshells around them
- Finding comfort when you are away from them

Reflect on your relationships and assess their patterns while answering these questions.

1. **Do you trust the people in your life?**
   o Yes
   o No

2. **Are you open and honest with each other?**
   o Yes
   o No

3. **Do you respect each other?**
   o Yes
   o No

4. **Do you support each other's efforts, passions, and dreams?**
   o Yes
   o No

5. **Is the relationship equal?**
   o Yes
   o No

6. **Do you feel comfortable expressing your thoughts and feelings?**
   o Yes
   o No

7. **Do you respect each other's space and independence?**
   o Yes
   o No

Healthy relationships can have a huge impact on every aspect of your life. According to a 2016 study conducted by Princeton University and Northwestern University, having a healthy social life can improve your mental and physical health and increase your lifespan.

Surround yourself with people who improve your life and teach you to trust others again. Take the step that changes your life and learn to establish strong and healthy relationships.

How to Develop a Healthy Relationship

After everything you have been through, you probably can't imagine what it feels like to be in a healthy relationship. You haven't learned to trust, love, and feel safe around people. However, it's never too late to open your heart up and allow yourself to love and be loved.

Know Yourself

Before you can establish healthy relationships, you should first know yourself. Take your time to discover who you truly are away from your past and pain. Try journaling or meditation to get in touch with your emotions. This will help you express yourself clearly and easily to avoid misunderstandings and conflicts.

People who don't truly know themselves struggle with regulating their emotions, which can affect their relationships and mental health.

Know What You Want

What does your ideal healthy relationship look like? How do you want to be treated in romantic relationships? What do you expect from your partner? What can you offer to strengthen the relationship and help it grow?

You and your partner should be clear on your needs, boundaries, aspirations, and goals. Remember, you are two different people with different interests, experiences, and backgrounds who came into this relationship with their expectations, hopes, and dreams.

You can't expect your partner to figure out what you want by themselves. You both should be open with each other and able to discuss your future goals in a safe space without fear of judgment.

One of the best ways to communicate your needs is to create a relationship vision board like the one in the image below.

A vision board is a collection of symbols, words, and images that concretize your objectives, hopes, and dreams in relationships, acting as a tangible reminder of what you are striving towards. It helps you and your partner connect and work together to build the future you have always wanted.

Create a relationship vision board to motivate you towards your goals.
Attribution-NonCommercial 2.0 Generic, CC BY-NC 2.0 DEED
<https://creativecommons.org/licenses/by-nc/2.0/>https://www.flickr.com/photos/sharisberries/25118543558

Before creating a vision board, you and your partner should get to know each other's strengths and weaknesses. This will help you align your relationship goals.

Reflect on your partner and your relationship and answer these questions.

1. What makes your partner happy?

_____
_____
_____
_____
_____
_____
_____
_____
_____

2. What triggers their anger?

_____
_____
_____

_____
_____
_____
_____
_____
_____

3. How do they act when they are under pressure?

_____
_____
_____
_____
_____
_____
_____

4. What do they hate?

_____
_____
_____
_____
_____
_____
_____

5. What do they like?

_____
_____
_____
_____
_____
_____
_____
_____

6. How do they relate to each other?

_____
_____
_____
_____
_____
_____
_____
_____
_____

After you finish, show your partner your answers and discuss them together. Then, let them answer the same questions about you and discuss their answers.

Tips Before Creating a Vision Board

- Set a timeframe for each goal. For instance, plan to have a baby in three years or own a house in two years.
- Decide whether your vision board is for your short-term or long-term goals. For instance, the board can be for short-term goals like annual vacations or date nights for long-term goals like starting a family.
- Decide what categories you want your board to focus on, such as hobbies, finances, career, health, or relationship goals. You can choose one or more categories. For instance, you can have health goals where you and your partner can adopt a healthy lifestyle to lose weight and become more active.
- Be specific and clear about your goals. Have an open conversation with your partner and discuss what your relationship is lacking. Perhaps you want to make more time for each other or get your finances under control.
- After deciding on your goals, find images to add to your board. For instance, if you want to start a family, put a picture of a baby. Or, if you want to go on a romantic trip to Paris, add a picture of the Eiffel Tower.
- You can also add symbols to your vision board. For instance, you can add an infinity sign to represent that your love and commitment to each other are infinite.

- Add affirmations to your board to keep you motivated and inspired. For instance, next to the baby's picture, you can write, "Our child will be smart, creative, and strong." Or you can write next to the house's picture, "We are close to living in our dream home."

- Organize your vision board and divide it into categories. You can also add a picture of you and your partner in the middle as a reminder that your main goal is to strengthen your relationship.

- Remember, this is a fun activity, so enjoy yourself. Don't be hard on yourself if it doesn't turn out how you want.

- The road to achieving your goals can be challenging, and you may feel emotionally drained. Stay motivated by constantly reminding yourself of your main purpose, such as loving each other, staying healthy, or creating a strong relationship. Write any of these statements in bold and add them to your visual board.

Instructions:

1. Get a corkboard or a poster board from Target or Amazon.
2. Search online and in magazines for images, symbols, and words representing your aspirations and goals.
3. When you find the right ones print them or cut them out from the magazines.
4. Pin them on your board.
5. Hang the board somewhere visible in your home. Take a picture of it and save it on your phone so you can access it.

Remember that the main goal of a vision board is to communicate with your partner and work together to create the future you both want.

Work on Your Goals

Now that you have determined your goals, start working towards them together. You should both put in the effort and time to build the relationship you want.

Learn to Trust

Trust doesn't come easy for people with disorganized attachments. If you are suspicious of your partner, friend, or co-worker, ask yourself whether they have done something to prompt this suspicion or if your trauma is affecting your judgment.

Ask for Help

Healthy relationships involve supporting one another. Understandably, asking for help can be hard for disorganized attachers. However, some people in your life will jump at the chance to support you and be there for you. Asking someone for help encourages them to come to you when they need assistance. This creates a balanced relationship that involves give and take.

Express Gratitude

Appreciate your loved ones by constantly expressing gratitude for everything they do for you. Say "thank you" whenever your co-worker helps you with a task, buy your best friend a gift to show appreciation for helping you move, or make your partner breakfast in bed to let them know you are grateful for their love and support.

Although you shouldn't wait for a thank you for helping your loved ones, they should still show appreciation for what you do for them. A lack of gratitude or appreciation is a huge red flag.

Fight with Love

Conflicts are inevitable in any relationship. How you handle them can either strengthen or break your relationship. Thinking clearly during arguments or handling the situation maturely can be difficult. However, remember that you are still on the same team, even if you are fighting.

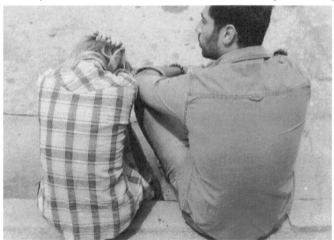

You're going to have fights, but make sure you address them with maturity and love at the end of them.

Give the other person the chance to express their feelings. Even if you don't agree with them, listen without interruptions to understand their side. Try to find a solution together. If either of you feels emotionally overwhelmed and unable to control your reactions, step back and go for a walk or to another room to calm yourself down. This will allow you to think clearly and regulate your emotions, giving you new insights and a fresh perspective.

Accept Your Differences

People are constantly changing and growing. Embrace your and their differences, even when you don't see eye to eye. Accept others for who they are without judgment. Understand that you complement each other with your different strengths and weaknesses. Appreciate the other person's different perspectives and values. Celebrate your uniqueness, and don't change for anyone.

Listen Actively

Nowadays, most people don't listen to what others are saying. They are either distracted by their phones or waiting for their turn to speak. Healthy relationships involve active listening, where you give the other person your full attention. You don't always have to respond or give your opinion. Sometimes, they only need a sympathetic ear.

Active listening allows you to know each other better and create strong bonds.

Set Healthy Boundaries

Setting boundaries lets people know how you want to be treated, which behaviors are acceptable, and which ones you won't tolerate. For instance, some people are uncomfortable with hugging so you should respect their boundaries by greeting them with a handshake or a nod.

Boundaries protect your personal space, safety, and physical and mental health. You should explain to your family, friends, co-workers, etc., that they are non-negotiable and should be respected.

Your loved ones will respect your needs and make you feel comfortable and safe around them. However, toxic individuals will keep pushing and testing you to see what they can get away with and if they can cross your boundaries.

Setting boundaries is simple; just follow these tips.

- Self-reflect to determine your boundaries. Find which actions and behaviors make you feel safe and which ones make you uncomfortable.

- Start with small and simple boundaries that you can easily implement before moving to complex ones. For instance, you can start by setting physical boundaries before setting sexual ones.
- Set boundaries early in the relationship.
- Set boundaries with everyone, like your partner, family, friends, co-workers, boss, and even your children.
- Explore each boundary and ask yourself if you feel content and safe with it or not. If you don't, adjust it.
- Communicating your boundaries can be uncomfortable. However, you need to consider how they will improve your relationships and life.
- When communicating your boundaries, be clear, direct, and firm. Explain to others how you prefer to be treated and why.
- Be consistent when reinforcing your boundaries, and make it clear that crossing them isn't an option.
- When someone crosses your boundaries once, explain to them how you feel and give them a second chance.
- If someone constantly tries to cross your boundaries, consider cutting them off, as they are most likely toxic individuals who don't respect you.
- Respect other people's boundaries just like you want them to respect yours.

Practice Empathy

Empathy is the ability to put yourself in someone else's shoes to feel what they are feeling, understand their thoughts, and sympathize with them. For instance, your co-worker is sad because her husband left her. You know that he abused and cheated on her, and she should be grateful for getting rid of him.

An empathetic person will try to see things from her perspective and recognize her pain. They won't minimize her experience, judge her, or try to change her feelings. Instead, they will make her feel heard and understood and validate her feelings to make her feel accepted.

If this was your co-worker, how would you respond to her?

_____
_____
_____
_____

How would you validate her feelings?

_____
_____
_____
_____

If you are tempted to say that she is better off, how would you reframe these thoughts and say something helpful and empathetic instead?

_____
_____
_____
_____

Say you are having lunch with your partner and their family. Out of nowhere, their brother makes fun of their stagnant career. You notice your partner looking embarrassed and angry, but they don't respond. You get home, and they still look upset.

How do you think your partner is feeling?

_____
_____
_____
_____

Do you feel they have the right to be upset in this situation?

_____
_____
_____
_____

How do you think you should approach them?

_____
_____
_____
_____

Although you may be tempted to comment on their brother's behavior, wait until your partner approaches you. If they don't, ask questions to get them to open up. You can say, "I noticed you got upset by your brother's comment; how did you feel when he said those words?"

Once they start talking, refrain from judgment or giving your opinion; just listen.

Say your best friend calls you crying because she has just lost her job and doesn't know what to do.

What should you tell your best friend to comfort them?

_____
_____
_____
_____

Will you ask them to come over to talk or just talk on the phone?

_____
_____
_____
_____

Will you comfort them with your words or hug them?

_____
_____
_____
_____

How do you feel about the way you handled the situation?

_____
_____
_____
_____

Is there anything more you wish you could have done?

_____
_____
_____
_____

Key Takeaways

- Healthy relationships are built with respect, honesty, and trust.
- Work with your partner to create relationship goals and aspirations.
- Practice gratitude and appreciate what your loved ones do for you.
- Set boundaries and be strict when someone crosses them.
- Practice empathy and put yourself in other people's shoes.

No relationship is perfect. Your goal isn't to avoid conflict and disagreements but to learn to handle these tough situations while still maintaining your love and respect for each other.

Section 9: Resilience: Thriving Beyond Attachment

According to modern scientific literature, resiliency is the ability to develop and sustain an efficient system to overcome or withstand the adversities that threaten this system. Based on the previously proposed model of resilience, the concept can be broken down into three fundamental elements:

- **Emotional reactivity** – incorporating sensitivity and intensity of reaction, recovery time needed, and impairment while emotional
- **Sense of relatedness** – comfort, trust, and perceived access to support from others
- **Sense of mastery** – entailing optimism, self-efficacy, and ability to learn from one's mistakes

Emotional reactivity can also be a risk factor, making it more likely that negative experiences will impair growth and development. Meanwhile, the sense of relatedness and mastery are protective factors within the concept of resilience because they reduce the chances that negative experiences will adversely affect personal growth and development. One of the experiences they can buffer against is unhealthy attachment.

Unhealthy attachment is possible to overcome with the right tools – and you can have a healthy relationship with your loved ones.

https://www.pexels.com/photo/portrait-of-happy-young-woman-using-mobile-phone-in-city-254069/

People with disorganized attachment often have trouble establishing a career or maintaining social connections due to higher emotional reactivity. For the same reason, to thrive beyond attachment, you must reduce the risk factor and develop the protective factors of a sense of relatedness and mastery. By helping you uncover your innate capacity to overcome challenges and fostering a mindset of strength and perseverance, this chapter will help you do just that — it will guide you on a journey of becoming a more resilient version of yourself.

Attachment, Resilience, And Coping

While resilience can protect you from stressful situations, your coping skills determine how you deal with them. Coping entails both cognitive and behavioral skills. In other words, how you navigate challenging situations stems from the coping strategies formed through your cognitive skills (your mind). You then act on the thoughts describing these strategies. The strategies are activated based on your ability to appraise the situation, your resources, and your emotional state at the time of the event.

Studies have determined that a parallel can be drawn between the attachment issues caused by early life experiences and the lack of resilience (Darling Rasmussen et al., 2019). Secure attachment shows a positive correlation with resilience. In the same vein, research indicates that resiliency and coping are also interconnected (Chen et al., 2019). Based on these, scientists assert that the availability of social support can act as a protective factor and lead to the development of effective coping strategies (Van der Hallen et al., 2020). Moreover, meaning-focused coping (derived from support-seeking) acts as a buffer between adversities and a person's well-being.

Studies have shown a positive correlation between problem-solving self-sufficiency and positive thinking (Li et al., 2018). In other words, optimism and self-sufficiency can help you hone cognitive and behavioral efforts, including positive thinking and problem-solving.

A recent study has demonstrated the interconnectedness of attachment, resilience, and coping (Godor et al., 2023). It asserts that you can trace the roots of how a person learns to manage stressors back to the elementary aspects of resiliency. These are, in turn, learned through interactions with the person's caregivers in childhood. The person develops an internal working model for navigating life based on these early social interactions.

Unfortunately, the building block that would foster an efficient working model is faulty in those who carry on unhealthy attachment patterns from childhood. However, this doesn't mean they can't rebuild it as adults. How you cope with a situation can be changed by altering your developed resilience factors. By exploring the polarities of trust and support, blocking and acknowledging emotions, self-reliance, and reliance on others, or moving toward deeper connections and moving away from them, you can make reliance a protective factor that'll help you thrive beyond attachment.

Resilience can be thought of as a muscle. In the same way that exercise can help you grow and strengthen your muscles, building reliance can help you navigate life's hurdles. It will encourage you to improve your adaptability, develop a positive outlook on life, and empower your overall well-being. You can use practical strategies to build your resilience muscle — and these strategies can help you become more resilient in the face of adversity.

Resilience Journal

Many people feel stuck in the face of adversity because they become fixated on the problem instead of seeking a resolution to it. By doing so, they self-sabotage their beliefs about themselves, catastrophizing the situation. Have you ever felt that a challenge is so big that you'll never overcome it? Or that this is the way it must be? A quick tip: by changing these beliefs, you can move forward and thrive, no matter how impossible the challenge may seem.

The trouble is, when you're dealing with deeply ingrained issues like unhealthy attachment style, you can't see your mistaken beliefs. If you could, you would be able to bounce back more easily.

Journaling has the power to help you navigate life through adversities despite your attachment issues. It's a practice rooted in techniques designed to calm and center your mind, enabling you to see the negative thoughts in black and white. Journaling allows you to put your thoughts on paper, read them over, discover the limiting patterns of belief, and take steps to change them.

Your resilience journal will be an incredible tool to foster your resilience and become a more empowered and confident version of yourself. If you are wondering how to begin your journal, here are a few prompts to consider:

- Have you already encountered something similar? In what ways did you handle them? Finding motivation for strengthening your resilience can be improved by knowing the answer to this query. Identify a scenario comparable to what you are going through right now.

- What happened during the previously described situation, and what was your first response? How did you resolve the issue?

- What allowed you to overcome the situation, and what did you learn from it?

- How has this obstacle contributed to your development? Has it helped you grow stronger, wiser, and more caring? What impact did it have on who you are now?

- Do you think the outcome as a whole was unsuccessful? Why, if so? How do you perceive failure? For instance, you might have been informed that you'll fail if you are not flawless throughout your life. This notion may cause you to give up on objectives that you otherwise think would be worthwhile.

- Consider how to change your views on failure. Why does it have to be a bad thing? Everyone, even the best, fails from time to time.

- How could you use failure as motivation to keep moving forward? Do you have someone who has achieved their goals thriving on their talents and skills? Have they failed beforehand?

- What made you resilient when faced with hardship in the past? Was it the network of people who supported you? Your capacity to grow from errors? A particular strategy or method you've employed (such as stress-reduction meditation, for example)

- What calms your mind and body? For example, do you find a chore or hobby particularly relaxing? Why do you enjoy these? Could you use these to focus on becoming more resilient in the face of adversity?

- Do you need to expand your support network and ask for additional help? If so, don't be afraid to admit it and reach out to friends, support groups, and professionals.

- Did your previous mistakes help you better understand what you wanted from a relationship? Did they make it clearer to you what you really wanted to accomplish in life?

- How do you want to be? Someone willing to fail, learn, and bounce back or someone who hides from challenges?

- How can you get closer to where you want to be?

- You are free to consider as many of the questions as you like. When replying to them, take your time and include as much information as you can. Who knows what insights you might have while writing?

An Egg, a Carrot, and the Coffee Beans

A young woman called an old friend, complaining about the difficulties she was facing in her life and stating she was on the verge of giving up. She said she was having problems with her partner because they were always fighting. On top of that, she felt that her boss and colleagues weren't appreciating the hard work she put into her job. The friend invited her over to talk about her problems.

As soon as she arrived, the friend invited her into the kitchen. Then, she filled three small pots with water, put them on the stove, and brought them to boil. When the water in all three pots was boiling, she poured coffee beans into the first, an egg into the second, and a carrot into the third. The friend let all three pots boil for 20 minutes without explaining what she was doing. Then, she removed the pots from the stove and took the carrot and the egg from their water, placing them in two separate bowls. Finally, she poured the coffee into a cup and put it in front of the young woman, along with the carrot and the egg.

Turning to the woman, the friend asked her what she saw in front of her. Confused, the woman said she could see an egg, a carrot, and coffee. Then, the friend gave her the egg and told her to peel it and see how it looked inside. The woman noted that it was hard. The friend also gave her the carrot to see how touching it felt. The woman noted that it was soft. Lastly, the friend told the woman to take a sip of the coffee, to which the woman noted how rich it tasted.

Still not understanding what her friend was trying to say, the woman asked what this meant. To this, her friend explained that the egg, the carrot, and the coffee beans went through the same hardship - being boiled in water. However, each had a different reaction to it. Namely, the egg had a hard but fragile shell and a liquid interior, but it became hard on the inside after being boiled. The carrot was hard, but it became soft and weak after boiling. The coffee beans, however, didn't change after being boiled in the water — instead, they changed the water.

Then, the friend asked the young woman how she would respond to challenges. Is she the egg that starts with a soft inside protected by a fragile shell and hardens after hardships? Is she a carrot that looks strong and unrelenting but becomes soft and powerless after a painful experience? Or is she like the coffee beans that use their inner power to change their circumstances? You can ask yourself the same questions.

The lesson: Adversity can be an extraordinary teacher if you're willing to reflect on what you've learned when facing it. You can use this knowledge to fortify your resilience. Remember, failures are part of life, and resilience is about learning to bounce back from and thrive beyond them. The more you practice building a resilient mindset, the closer you'll get to this goal.

Tip: Practicing self-care and mindfulness, developing coping strategies and a growth mindset, and building healthier relationships will help you enhance the empowering effects of facing adversities. It will also take your resilience to another level, rendering you capable of navigating any curveball life throws at you.

The Resilience Circle

This exercise is designed to help you identify and write down the people, activities, and beliefs that contribute to your resilience. This visual tool is a reminder of the support systems and personal values that empower them to thrive.

Draw a circle, and fill it with the following activities:

- Do something that makes you happy.
- Hug yourself.
- Think about all the positive things you have in your life.
- Be brave by trying something you haven't done before.
- Eat well and drink enough water.
- Get enough rest and sleep better.
- Engage in physical activity you enjoy.
- Write down the names (or draw the portraits) of those who care about you.
- Take deep breaths and count to 10.

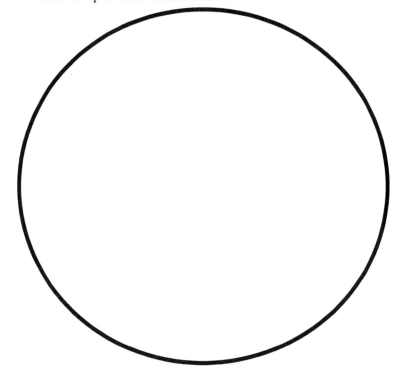

You decide where to put each activity within the circle. A quick tip: By putting the most helpful ones at the outer part of the circle, you give them more space, which also translates to importance. Therefore, start with the activities around the circle line if they help you strengthen in the face of hardship.

Once you've finished creating it, you can start using the resilience circle. Anytime you need a little support, choose a reassuring activity that helps you, and do it.

The Power of Community

One day, a donkey fell into a well. Hearing its cries for help, two other donkeys arrived at the well. Noticing a heap of sand next to the well, they kicked at it with their hind legs, throwing sand into the well. At first, the sand would fall on the head and back of the poor donkey inside the well, but it would soon start to shake it off. As the donkey continued to shake off the sand, it started piling up beneath his feet. The other two continued to kick the sand, and eventually, the pile inside became so high that the trapped donkey reached the top of the well and could hop out of it.

As you can see, support can go a long way toward helping you develop resilience. Cultivating meaningful relationships means you'll always have where to turn when you lack resilience in the face of adversity.

Future-Self Visualization

If you've decided to feed the wolf that represents positive emotions, it's time to visualize what this will bring you in the future. By imagining and describing your future self, living a life shaped by resilience and healthy attachments, you'll be encouraged to set goals and envision a future where you have successfully navigated beyond your attachment-related challenges.

Instructions:

1. Find a comfortable position, close your eyes, and take a deep breath.
2. Set your intention to visualize your future self. Your mind tends to naturally discount future events and focus only on the present. Make sure you won't have any distractions that would hinder your focus.

3. Acknowledge and discard thoughts of the present and past that may bubble up. This will help you orient yourself in the projected future scene.

4. Bring up a scene from the future. Focus on the image that clearly shows a positive change you've implemented since the present time. Or, it could depict you successfully overcoming a hardship. Try to bring as many details into this mental image.

5. Stay with this image for several minutes, observing its details, everything that happens, and how it happens. Engage your senses, too. Pick up on anything you can see, hear, smell, or taste.

6. When you're ready, release the image from your mind and slowly open your eyes.

Tips for making this exercise successful:

- Your decisions are driven by the same part of the mind affected by your emotions. Your feelings often have a much greater effect on your behavior than your rational thoughts. To get the empowering benefits of future self-visualization, actively embrace all the emotions as you observe the projected image.

- A crucial element of emotionally driven actions in future events is your ability to create a vivid image. How active your imagination is when capturing the image determines whether you can make the projected future into reality.

- Try to focus on a relatively close event. This will help your imagination become more vivid - and you'll have better chances of living in that future.

- When creating a mental image of your future self, think of it as if it's already a reality — as if you're already the person you see yourself to be in the future. This will create a vital connection to the future and be motivation to work toward the desired future.

Resilience Makes Goals Worth Pursuing

A grandmother was telling a story to her grandson. The story was about two wolves fighting with each other. One of the wolves was full of bad emotions, like anger, greed, fear, envy, regret, sadness, guilt, false pride, resentment, and ego-fueled actions like lies and seeing others as inferior. The other wolf was filled with good emotions like love, joy, peace, humility, hope, kindness, empathy, compassion, and benevolent actions that severed the truth and relationships. The tale continued about the endless fight between the two wolves. Finally, the grandson asked his grandmother which wolf would win the fight. The grandmother then smiled and said that the winner would be the wolf that gets fed the most — for these two live and fight a battle inside every person.

This is why a positive mindset is crucial for building resilience. It enables you to reframe negative experiences into growth opportunities. By focusing on the positive aspects of your circumstances, you can build a positive thought pattern more conducive to handling dress effectively.

In any pursuit, it has always been the journey that allows you to achieve happiness and fulfillment. Sometimes, the road on this journey is full of bumps — but what will always help you get back on track is resilience. When you reach your goals and victories (no matter how big or small), resilience will allow you to say, "I was able to get there despite everything."

Resilience will help you find enough happiness to make you thrive, enough trials to make you strong, and enough hope to make you happy. The happiest people don't always have the best of everything. However, they know how to make the most of every circumstance, whether good or bad. You can't move forward until you let go of the past hurts. Once you do that, you'll be able to become the strongest and most courageous version of yourself.

Section 10: Building a Supportive Community

Finally! You made it to the last chapter. Look at you go! You've felt all kinds of feelings throughout this journey and chose to stay on this growth path. That is so impressive. Not that you should be trying to impress anyone. You should be proud of yourself. Many others started this journey and backed out just when the finish line was in view. You're the true definition of a champion. Well done! Time to focus on building a community to help sustain and empower your growth.

Surround yourself with people that help you grow.

What if you were in a world where people wanted absolutely nothing to do with each other? A world where nobody bothered with forming and keeping communities? Everyone is solely responsible for themselves alone. That would be a boring world, for sure, not to mention the fact that there won't be a lot of children in such a world. So you probably wouldn't even be born because who knows? Maybe your grandparents don't speak to each other in this world; they were co-workers but never connected beyond hellos. Think about it for a moment. Life is never truly lived if you are completely alone.

Some people have lovely families, close blood relatives and all. If you are one of them, you should count yourself lucky. These people already have a strong support system, like a plush bed after a day of chaos all around. You lay down and it's as if your troubles and headache melt away when your head hits the pillow. They can even benefit from adding some friends to their group. Their families have given them a great head start.

Some families, however, aren't the best cheerleaders. Even as children, people from these homes never felt truly loved and cared for. Your healing process is not done until you have a solid, supportive community that will remind you of your greatness anytime you forget. The idea of building a community is a huge task. Most people say they don't know where to find good friends and support outside therapy. This final chapter will guide you on how to build a community if you don't have one yet, how to identify and recognize the one you have already but aren't conscious of, and how to strengthen your bonds. You are a winner; you'll need a team.

What Is a Supportive Community?

A supportive community is like a big group of friends and neighbors who are there for each other. They help out when someone needs it, like when a friend feels sad or is struggling. They offer words of encouragement and lend a helping hand when things get tough. Being part of a supportive community makes you feel like you belong somewhere. It's like having a big family who cares about and looks out for you. When you're part of a supportive community, you know you're not alone, and that's a comforting feeling.

In a supportive community, people understand each other's struggles and celebrate each other's successes. They listen when someone needs to talk and offer a shoulder to lean on when things are hard. Being surrounded by caring and understanding people helps you grow and feel good about yourself.

A supportive community is like a warm hug on a cold day—it makes you feel safe, loved, and valued. It's a place where you can be yourself and know you're accepted just as you are. Sounds like something you'd like to be part of, right?

Why Is Having a Supportive Community Important?

The best things in life aren't just about money, fame, and success. It's all about the friends we make and the people we care about. Having a strong group of people around you cannot be overestimated. They're like the strong base of a house, holding you up when you want to do things in life, whether at home, in school, or at work. They make you feel like you belong and help when things get tough. Why exactly should you bother with building a supportive system? Well, look at the numbers!

- A supportive community can provide emotional support; it can help you feel better when you're sad or worried. This support can come from friends, family, or even support groups.

- People in your community can understand and validate your feelings. They can help you feel like you're not alone in what you're going through.

- For someone with a disorganized attachment style, it can be hard to trust others. But having a supportive community can help you learn to trust again, as you see that they care about you and want to help.

- Being part of a supportive community can help you learn what healthy relationships look like. You see how others support each other and learn from their example.

- Knowing you have people caring for you can reduce your stress levels. You know that you have a safety net if things get tough.

- A supportive community can encourage you to keep going, even when things are hard. They motivate you to work on yourself and your healing journey.

- They can be your safe space. They make you feel safe and comfortable. When you're working on healing, things can feel confusing sometimes. Having friends who understand and don't judge lets you be open and honest, which helps you heal faster.
- A good friend group is like a practice squad. You can try healthy ways of connecting with them, like not hiding your feelings or asking for help. They'll be there to catch you if you mess up, and you can learn from each other.
- Disorganized attachment can make you feel like you don't quite fit in anywhere. A supportive group shows you, "Hey, you're welcome here!" It helps you feel secure and confident.
- Healing isn't always sunshine and rainbows. Sometimes it's rough. But with good friends, you don't have to go through it alone. They're your safety net, catching you before you fall too hard and crack some bones.

Community Mapping Exercise

Don't worry. You won't be asked to draw a map of a community. So relax. This isn't geography class. Community mapping exercise is like drawing a picture of all the people who are important to you. It's a simple way to see who is in your life and how they support you. Follow these steps to carry out the exercise.

Step 1: Gather Your Materials
- Take out a piece of paper, preferably large enough to accommodate multiple circles.
- Gather colored pencils, markers, or crayons to make your map colorful and clear.

Step 2: Create Your Community Map
- Find a quiet and comfortable space where you can work without distractions.
- Start by drawing a large circle in the center of your paper. This circle represents you, so add ears, eyes, nose, and a smile if you want.
- Around your circle, draw smaller circles to represent different people in your life. You can draw these circles randomly or organize them based on who they are to you: family, friends, teachers, or mentors.

Step 3: Identify Supportive Figures

- Think about the people who have been there for you during good and challenging times.

- These could be family members, like your parents, siblings, or grandparents. They could also be friends who make you laugh and cheer you up when you are feeling down.

- Write the names of these individuals inside the corresponding circles on your map.

- Include a brief note about how each person supports you to help you narrow your search down further.

Step 4: Add Details to Your Map

- Add some details to your map using different colors to distinguish between family members, friends, and other important figures in your life.

- Draw connecting lines or arrows between circles to show individual relationships or connections.

Step 4: Reflect on Your Support System

- Take a moment to review your completed map and reflect on the people you've included.

- Notice patterns in your support system. Are there certain individuals or groups who play a particularly significant role in your life?

- Consider how each person contributes to your overall well-being and sense of support.

Once you've finished your map, take a moment to look at it. You might be surprised by how many people are there for you. This exercise helps you realize you're not alone—you have a whole team of people cheering you on.

Step 5: Identify Areas for Growth

- As you examine your map, consider any gaps or areas where you could benefit from additional support.

- Are there relationships you'd like to strengthen or new connections you'd like to build?

- Use this reflection to think about ways to expand and add more people to your support network.

Step 6: Strategize Ways to Strengthen Your Community

Now that you've mapped out your community, how can you strengthen your connections with the people in your life?

- Brainstorm specific actions you can take to strengthen your connections with the people in your life.

- Spend more time with your family or reach out to someone who cares for extra help. This exercise helps you develop a plan to strengthen your support system.

- Consider contacting individuals you haven't connected with in a while, joining clubs or organizations where you can meet new people, or seeking mentors or role models who can offer guidance and support.

What Are the Benefits of This Exercise?

1. Drawing a map of your social network helps you see all the people who care about you.

2. It's like making a list of your cheerleaders and supporters. Seeing it visually can make you feel grateful and appreciated.

3. The community mapping exercise will help you better understand who is in your life and how they support you.

4. It's a simple but powerful tool for recognizing the people who matter most and strengthening your sense of belonging and support.

5. This awareness can be empowering as you recognize the positive influences in your life and acknowledge the support you receive.

6. This exercise can help strengthen your relationships by highlighting the importance of these connections and encouraging you to nurture them further.

7. The exercise can help alleviate feelings of loneliness and isolation often associated with disorganized attachment.

The Connection Plan - A Step-By-Step Guide

The connection plan helps you build stronger relationships and make new friends. It's a step-by-step guide to connecting with people who care about you and finding new supportive connections.

Step 1: Identify your goals. Think about what you want to achieve through your connections. Do you want to feel more supported? Make new friends? Improve existing relationships? Clarifying your goals will help you focus your efforts.

Step 2: Make a list. Write down the names of people you want to connect with or groups you want to join. This could include old friends, family members, or community organizations.

Step 3: Reach out. Take the first step by reaching out to those on your list. Send a text, make a phone call, or email to reconnect with old friends or family members. If you want to join a group or organization, look for opportunities to attend events or meetings.

Step 4: Be open and friendly. When you meet new people, be open to forming connections. Smile, ask questions, and show genuine interest in getting to know them. Building rapport takes time, so be patient and keep an open mind.

Step 5: Find common interests: Look for common interests or hobbies you share with others. Joining interest-based groups or clubs can be a great way to meet like-minded individuals and form meaningful connections.

Bonus step: Consider volunteering in your local community as a way to meet new people and give back. Volunteering allows you to make a positive impact and provides opportunities to connect with others who share similar values and interests.

Once you start taking proactive steps to strengthen existing relationships and form new connections, you can build a supportive network of people who uplift and empower you.

Picking Your Own Community

Describe the kind of individuals you wish to have around you. Use these sample traits to guide your reflection while shaping a profile of your desired connections. What qualities would you like to see in them?

How do they Appear Physically?

- Are you looking for someone who is athletic and enjoys sports activities?
- Do you prefer spending time with people who have a casual or more formal style?
- Would you like your friend to be affectionate and show warmth?

- Are you seeking companionship from someone who is single, married, or has children?

Who are they Emotionally?

- Do you value honesty, humor, and open communication in a relationship?
- Do you desire a relationship that is characterized by warmth and affection?
- Are you drawn to individuals who are easygoing and enjoy having fun?

What are their Spiritual Beliefs?

- Would you prefer someone who shares your religious beliefs or spiritual orientation?
- What are your thoughts on the spiritual beliefs of your potential friend?
- Is it important that your friend has a spiritual practice or belief system?

What are their Intellectual Abilities?

- Do you appreciate friends who are knowledgeable and well-read?
- What are your intellectual interests, such as politics or education?
- Are you looking for someone who shares similar intellectual pursuits?

How about Hobbies and Personal Interests?

- Do you value shared hobbies or interests in your friendships?
- What activities do you enjoy, such as gardening, theater, cooking, or crafts?
- Are you looking for someone who shares your hobbies or has complementary interests?

What are their Career and Financial Interests?

- Do you prefer friends who are passionate about their work or career pursuits?
- Consider the financial implications of your interests, such as travel expenses.

- Are you interested in sharing financial interests with your friends, such as investing or financial planning?

Gratitude Expression

You know that warm feeling you get when someone thanks you for something? Well, when you thank others, it makes you feel good too. Showing appreciation is one of the keys to fostering happiness for you and the person you're thanking. Gratitude expression is saying "thank you" to the people who make a difference in your life. It's how you show appreciation for the support and kindness you receive from others.

Make gratitude expression a part of your routine. Take a few minutes each day to think about someone in your community who has helped you or made you smile. Then, find a way to express your gratitude to them. Here are some ideas you can try:

Write a little note. Take a few minutes to write a quick "thank you" note to someone. It could be your neighbor who helped you bring in your groceries, the librarian who always finds the perfect book for you, or even the cashier at the store who always remembers your name. Even a simple "thank you for..." can brighten someone's day.

Send a quick message. Do you prefer texting or emailing? Sometimes, old-school feels more intimate. Use your phone or computer to send a message thanking someone for their help or kindness. A kind word can go a long way, even if it's just a few taps on your screen.

Do something nice. Remember, actions speak louder than words. Maybe you could help a neighbor with their yard work, offer to babysit for a friend, or bake cookies for the local fire station. Doing something small and thoughtful shows you care and strengthens the bonds between you and others.

Expressing gratitude has many benefits for both you and the people around you:

1. **It strengthens bonds.** When you say thank you, it shows the other person that you value them and their actions. This strengthens your bond with them and encourages them to continue being supportive.

2. **It brings about positive emotions.** Gratitude can make you feel happier and more content. Focusing on the good things in your

life and expressing appreciation for them boosts your mood and outlook.

3. **It reinforces support networks.** By expressing gratitude, you reinforce the importance of support networks. You acknowledge the people who are there for you and remind yourself of the positive connections you have.

Take a Look at Ben's Story:

Ben felt like he was trapped in a dark and lonely place with no hope of coming out. He carried the weight of his past on his shoulders, haunted by memories of a childhood marked by instability and fear. Growing up with disorganized attachment left the young man feeling disconnected and unworthy of love.

For several years, Ben believed he had to face his challenges alone. He built walls around himself, keeping others at arm's length to protect himself from further pain. But deep down, he longed for connection and support, yearning for someone to understand and accept him for who he truly was.

Therapy alone was not enough. Ben needed the support of his friends and family to truly heal. He gathered the courage to open up to them, and to his surprise, they responded with love and compassion, offering a shoulder to lean on and a listening ear.

As he leaned on his support network, he discovered the true meaning of strength. Ben learned that vulnerability was not a weakness but a source of power and resilience. With the unwavering support of his loved ones, he found the courage to confront his past and embrace a brighter future. He let go of the pain and shame that had held him back, embracing a newfound sense of hope and possibility.

Like Ben, you, too, will share your success story soon. Building a great group of friends takes time, sweat, and commitment. Don't get discouraged if it doesn't happen overnight. Finding the right people and building trust takes some getting to know each other. If you feel stuck or like people aren't connecting with you as you'd hoped, it might be time to brush up on your communication skills or take a deeper look at how you connect with others. Talking to a therapist can help here; they can offer tips and tricks to build stronger relationships.

When you find the right people, incorporate gratitude expression into your daily life. Don't ever forget to say "thank you." It can have a powerful impact on your well-being and relationships. It's a simple but meaningful way to show appreciation for the people who make a difference in your life and strengthen your sense of connection and community. Keep learning and growing. You're doing great.

Conclusion

Everything you went through while growing up has made you who you are now. Some of the things you learned when you were a child and how you learned to cope might be holding you back. Maybe something bad happened to you, or perhaps you grew up in a difficult home. As a result, you had tough thoughts and feelings that you're still dealing with as an adult. But it gets better, and since you're reading this last part, your growth process is already looking great.

Congratulations on reaching the end of your journey through the world of disorganized attachment and relationships with this book. What a journey it has been. From understanding the complexities of disorganized attachment to exploring how childhood experiences shape our connections, you've covered a lot of ground. It's been a wild ride.

You laughed, you cried, and you've learned a lot. You dug up memories and may even have laid a few to rest. Now, you understand the ups and downs of disorganized attachment relationships and how important it is to know yourself, trust others, talk openly, and be strong. You embarked on a self-discovery spree, exploring the depths of disorganized attachment and understanding how it affects you. You've learned to recognize the unhealthy patterns this attachment style can foster. No more masks.

This book has equipped you with all the tools to overcome the complexities of disorganized attachment. The activities and exercises were designed to help you explore the fertile ground of self-awareness and nurture the seeds of healing and inner peace. You have the power of communication to bridge the gaps between you and those around you.

And that is the best part. You're not alone! You also have amazing people who understand and share your goals and struggles. Be open and communicate with your loved ones. Having a supportive community can give you all the encouragement, understanding, and resources you need to continue growing and flourishing. Embrace the solace of self-compassion, learning to care for yourselves with the same tenderness you extend to others.

Keep everything you've learned about yourself through this journey at the forefront of your mind. You are a work in progress. Take advantage of the connections you made. Hold onto your new friends, the great things you discovered, and how much you've grown. You can create the kind of relationships and life you truly desire. Enjoy connecting with others, keep your friends close, and stay open to all the amazing things that can happen next. Cheers to you and the greatness that awaits you!

If you enjoyed this book, I'd greatly appreciate a review on Amazon because it helps me to create more books that people want. It would mean a lot to hear from you.

To leave a review:

1. Open your camera app.
2. Point your mobile device at the QR code.
3. The review page will appear in your web browser.

_____

Thanks for your support!

Here's another book by Andy Gardner that you might like

Free Bonus from Andy Gardner

Hi!

My name is Andy Gardner, and first off, I want to THANK YOU for reading my book.

Now you have a chance to join my exclusive email list related to human psychology and self-development so you can get the ebook below for free as well as the potential to get more ebooks for free! Simply click the link below to join.

P.S. Remember that it's 100% free to join the list.

Access your free bonuses here: https://livetolearn.lpages.co/andy-gardner-disorganized-attachment-workbook-paperback/

Or, Scan the QR code!

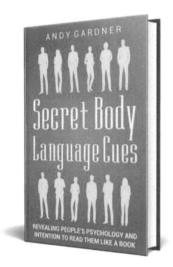

References

Brown, D. P., & Elliot, D. S. (2016). Attachment disturbances in adults: treatment for comprehensive repair. W.W. Norton & Company.

Cherry, K. (2021, December 2). Attachment Styles: Definition, Types, and Impact. Explore Psychology. https://www.explorepsychology.com/attachment-styles/

Cherry, K. (2022, May 26). The Different Types of Attachment Styles. Verywell Mind. https://www.verywellmind.com/attachment-styles-2795344

Drescher, A. (2023, June 19). Disorganized Attachment Style: Traits and Ways to Cope - Simply Psychology. Simply Psychology. https://www.simplypsychology.org/disorganized-attachment.html

Hunter, J., Maunder, R., & Le, T. L. (2016). Fundamentals of Attachment Theory. Improving Patient Treatment with Attachment Theory, 9–25. https://doi.org/10.1007/978-3-319-23300-0_2

Latif, S. (2021, April 20). Attachment Styles in Childhood: 6 Tips to Raise Secure & Happy Children. PositivePsychology.com. https://positivepsychology.com/attachment-styles-childhood/

Smith, M., Robbinson, L., Segal, J., & Reid, S. (2023, November 3). Attachment Issues in Children: Causes, Symptoms, Treatment - HelpGuide.org. Https://Www.helpguide.org. https://www.helpguide.org/articles/childhood-issues/attachment-issues-in-children.htm

The Attachment Project. (2020, July 2). Disorganized Attachment: Causes & Symptoms. Attachment Project. https://www.attachmentproject.com/blog/disorganized-attachment/

Bockarova, M. (2019, September 23). The Forgotten Attachment Style: Disorganized Attachment | Psychology Today. Www.psychologytoday.com. https://www.psychologytoday.com/intl/blog/romantically-attached/201909/the-forgotten-attachment-style-disorganized-attachment

Can mindfulness exercises help me? (2022, October 11). Mayo Clinic. https://www.mayoclinic.org/healthy-lifestyle/consumer-health/in-depth/mindfulness-exercises/art-20046356

Disorganized Attachment Style in Relationships: The Complete Guide. (n.d.). Attachment Project. https://www.attachmentproject.com/disorganized-attachment-relationships/

Drescher, A. (2023, October 28). Disorganized Attachment Style. Disorganized Attachment Style: Traits and Ways to Cope. https://www.simplypsychology.org/disorganized-attachment.html#The-Development-of-Disorganized-Attachment-Style

Green, R. (2023, June 20). How a Disorganized Attachment Style Impacts Relationships and How to Heal. Verywell Mind. https://www.verywellmind.com/disorganized-attachment-in-relationships-7500701

Knafo, H., Murphy, A., Steele, H., & Steele, M. (2018). Treating disorganized attachment in the Group Attachment-Based Intervention (GABI©): A case study. Journal of Clinical Psychology, 74(8), 1370–1382. https://doi.org/10.1002/jclp.22647

Li, A. P. (2020, October 5). Disorganized Attachment: Understanding How It Forms & How To Heal. Parenting for Brain. https://www.parentingforbrain.com/disorganized-attachment/#what

Moore, A. (2020, August 12). Disorganized Attachment: 9 Signs Of The Lesser-Known Attachment Style. Mindbodygreen. https://www.mindbodygreen.com/articles/disorganized-attachment

Moore, M. (2018, April 28). Disorganized Attachment Style: Signs, Causes, and Management. Psych Central. https://psychcentral.com/health/disorganized-attachment#definition

Robinson, L., Segal, J., & Jaffe, J. (2021, February). How Attachment Styles Affect Adult Relationships. HelpGuide.org. https://www.helpguide.org/articles/relationships-communication/attachment-and-adult-relationships.htm

Saxena, S. (2021, April 29). Disorganized Attachment: Definition, Causes, & Signs. Choosing Therapy. https://www.choosingtherapy.com/disorganized-attachment/

The Attachment Project. (2020, July 2). Disorganized Attachment: Causes & Symptoms. Attachment Project.

https://www.attachmentproject.com/blog/disorganized-attachment/

BetterHelp Editorial Team. (2024, February 22). Unhealthy Attachment Styles: Types, Definitions, And Therapy | Betterhelp. Www.betterhelp.com. https://www.betterhelp.com/advice/relations/unhealthy-attachment-styles-types-definitions-and-therapy/

Coelho, S. (2022, March 9). Journaling For Emotional Health: 12 Writing Prompts. Psych Central. https://psychcentral.com/blog/journal-prompts-to-heal-emotions#recap

Lancer, D. (2021, April 1). How to Change Your Attachment Style and Your Relationships | Psychology Today. Www.psychologytoday.com. https://www.psychologytoday.com/us/blog/toxic-relationships/202104/how-change-your-attachment-style-and-your-relationships

Marriage.com Editorial Team. (2023, February 16). 25 Signs of Unhealthy Attachment in Relationships. Marriage Advice - Expert Marriage Tips & Advice. https://www.marriage.com/advice/relationship/unhealthy-attachment-in-relationships/

Silva Casabianca, S., & Montijo, S. (2021, October 14). Have an Unhealthy Attachment to Your Partner? Healing Is Possible. Psych Central. https://psychcentral.com/blog/healing-unhealthy-relationship-attachments

Sutton, J. (n.d.). Anxious Attachment Patterns. https://positive.b-cdn.net/wp-content/uploads/2022/01/Anxious-Attachment-Patterns.pdf

Sutton, J. (2022, June 30). Attachment Styles in Therapy: 6 Worksheets & Handouts. PositivePsychology.com. https://positivepsychology.com/attachment-style-worksheets/

Brassart, S. (2022, June 27). Wounded Healers: Acknowledge and Address Emotional Wounds. Sex and Relationship Healing. https://sexandrelationshiphealing.com/blog/wounded-healers-acknowledge-and-address-emotional-wounds/

Dr. Sophia. (2020, January 1). 7 Ways to Heal Your Old Emotional Wounds. Www.thehappinessdoctor.com. https://www.thehappinessdoctor.com/blog/7-ways-to-heal-your-old-emotional-wounds

HAUCK, C. (2018, October 11). A 10-Minute Meditation to Work with Difficult Emotions. Mindful. https://www.mindful.org/a-10-minute-meditation-to-work-with-difficult-emotions/

Martin, S. (2019, March 22). 8 Tips for Healing Emotional Wounds. Psych Central. https://psychcentral.com/blog/imperfect/2019/03/8-tips-for-healing-emotional-wounds#Healing-Meditation

McBride, C. (2023, May 2). Addressing Emotional Wounds: The Hidden Key to Success and Well-Being.

Www.linkedin.com. https://www.linkedin.com/pulse/addressing-emotional-wounds-hidden-key-success-christopher-mcbride-sr/

Mogire, S. (2023, January 13). 10 Practical Ways Intelligent People Heal Emotional Wounds. Www.linkedin.com. https://www.linkedin.com/pulse/10-practical-ways-intelligent-people-heal-emotional-wounds-mogire/

Salters-Pedneault, K. (n.d.). How Accepting Emotions Can Improve Your Health. Verywell Mind. https://www.verywellmind.com/how-accepting-emotions-can-improve-emotional-health-425368#toc-how-to-practice-accepting-emotions

Tewari, A. (2022, March 23). 105 Healing Affirmations for Blissful Well-Being. Gratitude - the Life Blog. https://blog.gratefulness.me/healing-affirmations/

The Value of Acknowledging Your Pain | The Guest House. (2021, April 3). Www.theguesthouseocala.com. https://www.theguesthouseocala.com/the-value-of-acknowledging-your-pain/

Carter, Brittini. "4 Tips to Build Everyday Trust in Relationships." The Gottman Institute, 10 Aug. 2021, www.gottman.com/blog/4-tips-to-build-everyday-trust-in-relationships/.

Craig, Heather. "10 Ways to Build Trust in a Relationship - PositivePsychology.com." PositivePsychology.com, 10 July 2019, positivepsychology.com/build-trust/.

Hailey, Logan. "30 Best Trust-Building Exercises to Rebuild Relationships." Science of People, 22 Mar. 2023, www.scienceofpeople.com/trust-building-exercises/.

Spatz, Steven. "7 Important Tips to Build Trust in Relationships." Best Marriage Advice - Get Marriage Tips from Experts, Marriage.com, 24 Aug. 2018, www.marriage.com/advice/relationship/7-important-tips-to-build-trust-in-relationships/.

Ackerman, Courtney. "49 Communication Activities, Exercises, and Games." PositivePsychology.com, 27 May 2019, positivepsychology.com/communication-games-and-activities/.

Cherry, Kendra. "How to Improve Your Communication in Relationships." Verywell Mind, 23 Feb. 2022, www.verywellmind.com/communication-in-relationships-why-it-matters-and-how-to-improve-5218269.

McDermott, Nicole. "How to Communicate in a Relationship, according to Experts." Forbes Health, 12 Jan. 2024, forbes.com/health/wellness/how-to-communicate-in-a-relationship/.

Robbins, Tony. "The Key to Communication in Relationships." Tonyrobbins.com, 2019, www.tonyrobbins.com/ultimate-relationship-guide/key-communication-relationships/.

CapelDiego. (2024, January 24). "HealingSelfCriticism: TransformativeSelfCompassion for PersonalGrowth" | About Me Stories. Mirror-Medium.com. https://mirror-medium.com/?m=https://medium.com/about-me-stories/turning-self-criticism-into-self-compassion-54475d989422?source=rss----ee447970a50d---4

Dougherty, A. (2023, October 29). 20 Self-Compassion Quotes as Daily Affirmations. Medium. https://abbyedougherty.medium.com/20-self-compassion-quotes-as-daily-affirmations-e7f6d05432b8

Greenberg, M. (2019, March 31). Self-Compassion May Foster More Secure Attachment | Psychology Today. Www.psychologytoday.com. https://www.psychologytoday.com/us/blog/the-mindful-self-express/201903/self-compassion-may-foster-more-secure-attachment

Johnson, C. (n.d.). Writing a Letter to Your Younger Self–Care Counseling: Minneapolis Therapists. Care Counseling. https://care-clinics.com/writing-a-letter-to-your-younger-self/

Neff, K. (2015, February 23). Exercise 6: Self-Compassion Journal. Self-Compassion. https://self-compassion.org/exercise-6-self-compassion-journal/

SG, T. T. P. (2020, July 30). The Struggle for Self-Compassion: Karen's Story. THE TAPESTRY PROJECT SG. https://thetapestryproject.sg/the-struggle-for-self-compassion-karens-story/

Team. (2022, March 10). Be Kind to Yourself: Attachment & Self-Compassion. Attachment Project. https://www.attachmentproject.com/blog/be-kind-to-yourself/

The Doctor's Kitchen. (2022, November 14). Beautiful Story About Self Compassion! #shorts. Www.youtube.com. https://www.youtube.com/watch?v=qsrsrrN9Z1k

Blomquist, L. (2022, December 22). 5 Ways to Practice Empathy in Your Relationship. Brides. https://www.brides.com/practice-empathy-in-relationship-6951684

Cherry, K. (n.d.). Are Your Relationships Healthy? Here's How to Tell. Verywell Mind. https://www.verywellmind.com/all-about-healthy-relationship-4774802#toc-signs-of-unhealthy-relationships

Evans, J. (2024, January 8). Best Vision Boards for Couples: 110 Ideas & Examples (2024). Healthy, Happy, Impactful. https://healthyhappyimpactful.com/vision-boards-for-couples/

Melissa. (2022, December 2). How To Create A Couple's Vision Board. Elephant on the Road. https://www.elephantontheroad.com/how-to-create-a-couples-vision-board/

Perry, E. (2021, July 30). Setting Boundaries at Work and in Relationships: A How-To Guide. Www.betterup.com. https://betterup.com/blog/setting-boundaries

Perry, E. (2023, June 21). Healthy Relationships: 13 Valuable Tips. Www.betterup.com. https://www.betterup.com/blog/healthy-relationships-in-life

Top tips on building and maintaining healthy relationships. (2023). Mental Health Foundation. https://www.mentalhealth.org.uk/our-work/public-engagement/healthy-relationships/top-tips-building-and-maintaining-healthy-relationships

What Does a Healthy Relationship Look Like? (n.d.). Www.ny.gov. https://ny.gov/teen-dating-violence-awareness-and-prevention/what-does-healthy-relationship-look

Williams, N. (2022, October 27). 15 Vision Board Ideas for Couples to Improve Their Relationships. Marriage Advice - Expert Marriage Tips & Advice. https://www.marriage.com/advice/relationship/vision-board-for-couples/#15_vision_board_ideas_for_couples_to_improve_their_relationships

Yang, Y. C., Boen, C., Gerken, K., Li, T., Schorpp, K., & Harris, K. M. (2016). Social relationships and physiological determinants of longevity across the human life span. Proceedings of the National Academy of Sciences, 113(3), 578–583. https://doi.org/10.1073/pnas.1511085112

A Carrot, an Egg, and a Cup of Coffee - Transforming Lives Through Resilience Education. (n.d.). https://sites.edb.utexas.edu/resilienceeducation/inspiring-stories/a-carrot-an-egg-and-a-cup-of-coffee/

Doll, K. (2019, March 23). 23 Resilience Building Tools and Exercises (+ Mental Toughness Test). PositivePsychology.com. https://positivepsychology.com/resilience-activities-exercises/

Godor, B. P., van der Horst , F. C. P., & Van, R. (2023). Unraveling the Roots of Emotional Development: Examining the Relationships Between Attachment, Resilience and Coping in Young Adolescents. Journal of Early Adolescence, 44(4), 027243162311818-027243162311818. https://doi.org/10.1177/02724316231181876

Greater Emotional Resilience. (n.d.). FasterCapital. https://fastercapital.com/keyword/greater-emotional-resilience.html

Hailey Rodgers, H. (n.d.). Journaling for Resilience | The Journal That Talks BackTM. www.thejournalthattalksback.com. https://www.thejournalthattalksback.com/blog/journaling-for-resilience

Meier, J. (n.d.). How To Visualize Non-Attachment. Sources of Insight. https://sourcesofinsight.com/visualize-non-attachment/

Srilakshmi. (2017, May 29). Building emotional bonds with your future self. Www.linkedin.com. https://www.linkedin.com/pulse/building-emotional-bonds-your-future-self-srilakshmi-/?trk=article-ssr-frontend-pulse_more-articles_related-content-card

The Farmer and the Donkey - Transforming Lives Through Resilience Education. (n.d.). https://sites.edb.utexas.edu/resilienceeducation/inspiring-stories/the-farmer-and-the-donkey/

The Two Wolves - Transforming Lives Through Resilience Education. (n.d.). https://sites.edb.utexas.edu/resilienceeducation/inspiring-stories/the-two-wolves/

Twinkle. (2022). The Wheel of Resilience Activity. Twinkl.com. https://www.twinkl.com/resource/the-resilience-spin-wheel-activity-sheet-t2-p-535

Chen, H., Xu, J., Mao, Y., Sun, L., Sun, Y., & Zhou, Y. (2019). Positive Coping and Resilience as Mediators Between Negative Symptoms and Disability Among Patients With Schizophrenia. Frontiers in Psychiatry, 10(641). https://doi.org/10.3389/fpsyt.2019.00641

Darling Rasmussen, P., Storebø, O. J., Løkkeholt, T., Voss, L. G., Shmueli-Goetz, Y., Bojesen, A. B., Simonsen, E., & Bilenberg, N. (2018). Attachment as a Core Feature of Resilience: A Systematic Review and Meta-Analysis. Psychological Reports, 122(4), 1259–1296. https://doi.org/10.1177/0033294118785577

Folkman, S. (2013). Stress: Appraisal and coping. Encyclopedia of Behavioral Medicine, 1(1), 1913–1915. https://doi.org/10.1007/978-1-4419-1005-9_215

Li, M., Eschenauer, R., & Persaud, V. (2018). Between Avoidance and Problem Solving: Resilience, Self-Efficacy, and Social Support Seeking. Journal of Counseling & Development, 96(2), 132–143. https://doi.org/10.1002/jcad.12187

Van der Hallen, R., Jongerling, J., & Godor, B. P. (2020). Coping and resilience in adults: a cross-sectional network analysis. Anxiety, Stress, & Coping, 33(5), 1–18. https://doi.org/10.1080/10615806.2020.1772969

Community mapping and making connections. (n.d.). Perkins School for the Blind. https://www.perkins.org/resource/community-mapping-and-making-connections/

Focus on Healing. (2023, October 28). Healing Through Connection: Building a Supportive Community - Focus On Healing. Focus on Healing Wellness Institute. https://focusonhealing.com/healing-through-connection-building-a-supportive-community/

MacWilliam, B. (2022, June 6). How to Heal Disorganized Attachment in Adults. Attachment in Adult Relationships. https://brianamacwilliam.com/heal-disorganized-attachment/

Mell. (2019, February 9). How do you do community mapping exercises? –
Sluiceartfair.com. Www.sluiceartfair.com.
https://www.sluiceartfair.com/2019/users-questions/how-do-you-do-community-
mapping-exercises/

Miller, S. (2022, June 13). How to create a supportive community. Thrive
Global. https://community.thriveglobal.com/how-to-create-a-supportive-
community/

Nuwaira. (2023, June 30). Build a Supportive Community! - Life With
Nuwaira. Life with Nuwaira. https://www.nuwairalife.com/build-a-supportive-
community/blog/

Prasetyo, F. (2023, March 14). How To Heal From Disorganized Attachment:
The Ultimate Guide - Lifengoal. Lifengoal. https://lifengoal.com/how-to-heal-
from-disorganized-attachment/

Scott, K. (2023, September 11). 5 Simple Ways to Cultivate a Supportive
Community. Www.churchescare.com. https://www.churchescare.com/blog/5-
ways-cultivate-supportive-community

Walker, S. (2018, September 29). How to build a supportive community.
Psychologies. https://www.psychologies.co.uk/how-to-build-a-supportive-
community/

Zopian, H. (2023, March 21). Building a Supportive Community for Personal
and Physical Growth: 6 Steps to Success. Medium.
https://medium.com/@haldiszopian.md/building-a-supportive-community-for-
personal-and-physical-growth-6-steps-to-success-d884508b94f8

Made in United States
Troutdale, OR
10/07/2024

23503252R00086